SOFTBILLED BIRDS

SOFTBILLED BIRDS

Clive Roots

JOHN GIFFORD LTD · LONDON

Published in Great Britain
by John Gifford Ltd.
125 Charing Cross Road,
London, W.C.2.

S.B.N. 70710421 1

20.rP

Printed in Great Britain
by Compton Printing Ltd.,
London and Aylesbury, England.

Acknowledgements

The author gratefully acknowledges the assistance of Mr. R. Edgar Pye who provided the analysis of the insectile mixtures outlined on pages   . The photographs were taken by Robin Brown at the Winged World, Morecambe except where otherwise indicated, and are reproduced by permission of Morecambe Corporation. The food analysis on page 136 is reproduced from *The Composition of Foods* with the kind permission of the Controller of Her Majesty's Stationery Office.

Preface

The object of this book has been to provide information upon the practical aspects of maintaining softbills, and nutrition—the most important aspect—has been considered from an unusual angle where birds are concerned, as an attempt has been made to investigate their calorific requirements. Research on this subject has indicated that the diet of caged birds is probably richer than it should, or need be, and consequently both their life span and breeding potential are reduced. If a true pair of birds is available, breeding is after all primarily dependent upon diet, and secondly upon space and facilities.

A brief review of the families of softbilled birds is given in part II, but the intention has not been to provide detailed descriptions of these birds as an aid to identification, as this information is adequately provided by the many excellent field guides and handbooks which have been produced in recent years. In any case, one volume could certainly not do justice to the task of describing fully even those softbills that are common avicultural subjects.

Included in the appendixes is a table of the composition of the foods normally given to softbilled birds, from which it can be ascertained whether the diet provided is as suitable as it could be for a particular species. In addition it will assist in putting into their correct perspective the inherited assumptions such as the fact that mealworms are too "rich", apparently for all softbills; and that bananas are too fattening, which is true of course, yet sultanas and currants which have a far higher carbohydrate content, are often used liberally.

Clive Roots

Contents

PART I
The Acquisition and Care of Softbills

An Introduction to the Softbills

"Softbills" is a relatively new name for a group of birds recognised aviculturally and normally defined as cage and aviary birds with soft bills which feed upon nectar, insects or fruit. This is partly correct, although "feeding upon soft plant material" would be more appropriate, as many species do not confine themselves to fruit and nectar in the wild but also eat shoots, leaves, flowers, berries and even plant sap. Also, the insectivorous species take other arthropods such as crabs, crayfish and spiders in addition to insects, and are not averse to including amphibians, reptiles, fish and even warm-blooded animals in their diet. Some, like the fish-eating kingfishers, are restricted to a carnivorous diet and live solely upon aquatic vertebrates. The kookaburra and others prey mainly upon terrestrial vertebrates. Yet the diverse feeding habits of these birds should not exclude them from the softbills. In any case the fish-eating kingfishers are generally regarded as a recent development from the insectivorous species, and there are many still in the intermediate stage which feed upon insects and aquatic vertebrates. The land-dwelling forms obviously find it more economical to include fleshier vertebrates in their otherwise insectivorous diet.

On the basis of diet however it would obviously be in order to include the pheasants, roulrouls, tinamous and others which exist mainly upon berries and insects in the wild; and the waders too, as they are as insectivorous as most kingfishers. All these are recognised "aviary" birds, yet it would be nonsensical to call them softbills, so where de we draw the line?

The relative softness of a bird's bill is no criterion either, as the beaks of many birds designated softbills are virtually as hard as those of the seed-eaters and the birds of prey, although as a general rule they are not adapted for cracking seeds or tearing flesh. Members of the Corvidae are exceptions as they are able to hold food items with their feet to assist in tearing and pulling, and are quite adept at dealing with carrion. Birds of the genus Quiscalis have specialised jaw muscles and a keeled upper mandible which allow them to open nuts, while the hard bills and modified muscles of the true woodpeckers enable them to drill into hard wood and to split nuts. These species therefore have harder bills than many accepted aviary birds such as the jacanas, stilts and thicknees, which although they fit the old definition are certainly not softbills. The hard-billed softbills mentioned above are of course exceptions and as any person who has handled birds will know, the bite of a tree pie does not compare with that of a nectar-eating parrot—lory—of similar size. Therefore if diet is accepted as one of the primary criteria when classifying the softbills, the degree of softness of the bill is certainly not conclusive. Neither is the fact that species are cage or aviary birds in conjunction with bill and diet sufficient limitation, as the pheasants, partridge and waders are also aviary birds. We cannot exclude these birds, at least the pheasants and roulroul, by restricting softbills to those birds which roost in trees at night irrespective of their daytime habits, as both they and the trumpeters and curassows are more arboreal than the pittas, rock thrushes and larks.

In addition to their diet, relative softness of bill and suitability for cage or aviary life, softbills can be restricted to a workable group by considering the state of the young upon hatching, and for the purpose of this book softbills are:
"Cage and aviary birds with relatively soft bills, which feed upon insects* and soft plant material and whose young are helpless at birth."

The young of the majority of species are naked when they hatch, but some have a light covering of down at birth and a few are densely covered. Jacamar nestlings are examples of the

*Footnote "including larger animal prey"

latter as they are clad in long white down when they hatch, and the young of the sun bittern also resemble nidifugous chicks in that respect only.

The keeping of any bird in confinement presents problems of acceptance and compatability when attempts are made to provide a mate for a single specimen, or add more individuals to quarters already housing a pair or group which have had time to establish their territorial boundaries. Where the smaller softbills are concerned the problems are magnified as it is not always possible to house a single pair of birds per aviary or flight, either economically where the private aviculturist is concerned, or to provide value for money for the paying zoo or bird garden visitors. The result is therefore a predominance of mixed groups in which compatability is the key factor, and when dealing purely with softbills it is more difficult to achieve good results than when a comprehensive collection is maintained, and quail, finches, small parakeets and similar birds can be included.

Softbills are usually grouped together according to size, and in many cases the behaviour of commonly kept species can be forecast fairly accurately, although allowance must always be made for individual variations of course. Known aggressive species such as shamas, long-tailed glossy starlings, white-crested jay thrushes, cissas, blue magpies, cocks of the rock and toucans should only be accommodated with birds of equal size, or even larger if they are particularly docile species.

Often, however, compatability is dependent upon the size of the cage or compartment, rather than the similarity in size of the birds. The larger the area, and particularly the height, available to the birds the greater can be the size variation of the species accommodated. The ultimate are the large planted tropical houses, in which can be kept birds ranging in size from hummingbirds to toucans, the smaller species being safe as they will frequent the lower levels of the vegetation, while the larger species use the highest branches and come down only to feed. Obviously the larger predatory species would not be included in such an arrangement.

In many instances known aggressive species tolerate smaller birds if all are introduced into new quarters at the same time. In this way both species of cock of the rock have been housed, in planted aviaries approximately 20 by 12 ft., with green-backed tits, black-headed honeycreepers, D'Arnauds barbets and many other small softbills. In no circumstances would this apply to the cissas or blue magpies however.

Flock birds, in which the social habit is highly developed, are obviously the best subjects for community aviaries. The fruit pigeons, honeycreepers, smaller tanagers, bee-eaters and similar species are usually harmless to other species, however docile these may be.

The breeding of many species of softbilled birds for the first time in captivity is recorded every year, and the number will almost certainly increase annually as more knowledge is gained of their specialised food requirements and their breeding habits. Assuming that a compatible pair of birds is both established and acclimatised, the other requirements of the breeding pair are a correct diet, sufficient space, seclusion and nesting facilities, i.e. suitable sites and materials. The instances of softbills breeding in show cages are exceptions, and while there is some truth in the statement that birds will breed anywhere if they really want to, the fact remains that they are far more likely to breed if given sufficient space. A range of flights housing nesting pairs of softbills is not such an unusual sight these days, but the same cannot be said about a similar number of small cages. Seclusion is equally important. Although some birds may tolerate inoffensive species within their quarters when breeding, and allow occasional glimpses of their eggs or young, as a general rule birds lacking competition for food and territory, and undisturbed by humans, produce the best breeding results.

As with all aspects of bird-keeping the provision of a correct diet is vitally important, as birds will not come into breeding condition if their diet is deficient in certain nutrients, or too high in energy providing foods. Calcium is required by the adult bird for egg-shell formation, and a high protein intake is necessary to produce eggs. It will be seen in chapter 6 that it is very easy to overfeed avicultural subjects, not by the amount of food eaten, but the number of calories that the diet provides. The richness of bird's diets must of course be associated with the temperature at which they are kept, and not with the size of the cage or aviary in which they are housed, as the amount of exercise they get is still negligible compared with that of the wild bird.

Several softbills are in danger of extinction, particularly species restricted to small islands, and those which cannot adapt to the reduction or alteration of their habitat. Rothschild's grackle is one of these, but fortunately it is fairly well represented in captivity, and breeds with some regularity. Many softbills are rarer in collections than this species however and yet are fairly plentiful in the wild, and there are several reasons for this. First there are the species which are inaccessible to collectors due to natural hazards. The umbrella birds for instance are found in the wildest, often unexplored, territory of north western South America; and the same applies to the numerous species of cotingas which also frequent the forest canopy. Many species are protected in their country of origin and are seldom available even to the long established zoological gardens. The softbills of Australasia and Madagascar fall into this category. Others are protected by political boundaries, and the many species endemic to Cuba, China and Indonesia are seldom available to aviculturists.

Although there is little prospect of a viable captive breeding population of any softbill species acting as a safeguard against the possible extinction of the bird in the wild state, every compatible pair should of course be encouraged to nest, and when possible mates obtained for single birds. While many will construct their own nests if provided with suitable materials, a large number require suitable sites or receptacles before they will attempt to nest. Well rotted, large diameter tree trunks or stumps should be provided for the barbets and woodpeckers which are able to drill their own holes, and any that are used for short periods and then discarded will be suitable for tits and nuthatches. Sturdily built nest boxes with a single entrance hole are of course the most easily provided type for the hole nesters, and similar boxes with the front half covered are suitable for starlings, mynahs and grackles among others. Tanagers and honeycreepers need small baskets unless there is sufficient dense cover in the form of small bushes for them to nest in. The nesting materials provided should be both for the basic nest construction—pliable twigs, coarse grass, raffia, palm fronds etc.; and for the lining horsehair, fine grass, cotton wool, mud and similar materials should be provided.

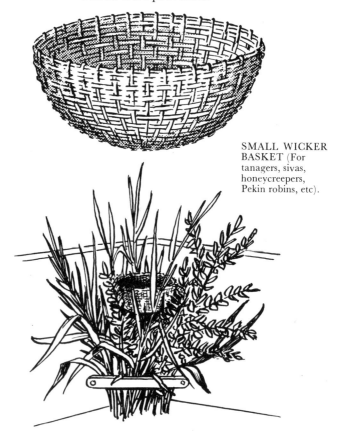

SMALL WICKER BASKET (For tanagers, sivas, honeycreepers, Pekin robins, etc).

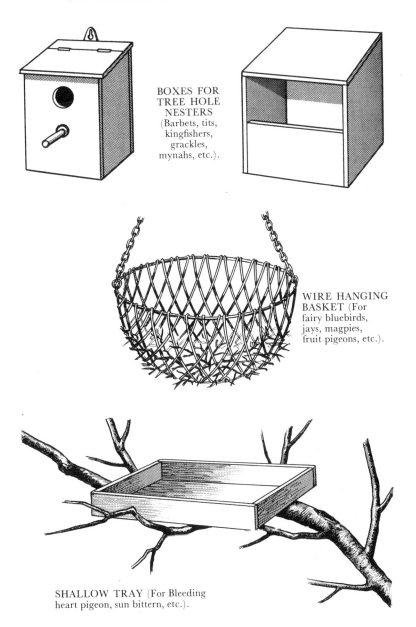

BOXES FOR
TREE HOLE
NESTERS
(Barbets, tits,
kingfishers,
grackles,
mynahs, etc.).

WIRE HANGING
BASKET (For
fairy bluebirds,
jays, magpies,
fruit pigeons, etc.).

SHALLOW TRAY (For Bleeding
heart pigeon, sun bittern, etc.).

Many species of softbills nest only once a year, but the number of clutches is to a certain extent dependent upon the availability of food; and several species have two, and even three, clutches per year in the tropics. With few exceptions, one of them being the roadrunner, incubation does not begin until the whole clutch has been laid, unlike the birds of prey. If a softbill remains on the nest during daylight hours before egg-laying is completed it does not necessarily mean that incubation has started. Unless the brood patches are exposed the bird's body heat will be conserved by its feathers.

The Acquisition of Softbills

According to the late Lee S. Crandall, for many years Curator of Birds at the New York Zoological Park, the birds of paradise caught for him during an expedition to New Guinea in 1929 were trapped with snares set in the fruiting trees in which the birds were accustomed to feeding, or around a bait of fruit elsewhere. The Papuan trappers often had to wait hours before a quick pull on the line secured a rare and beautiful specimen. In the same era professional bird trappers scoured the tropics for species which were often known only from a few skins in museums. These trappers were sometimes sponsored by wealthy landowners who had fantastic collections of birds on their estates.

Alas, the days of the zoo arranged collecting trips and free-lance trapping expeditions are practically over, hastened by the increase in the number of bird exporters operating in the tropics, and the ease and speed with which consignments of rare birds can be sent by air. Air transport has probably played the most important part in the decline as it has enabled exporters abroad to send many delicate species of birds which would not have survived a long sea journey unless accompanied by an expert en route.

Some of the birds available to aviculture however are still obtained in the time consuming manner in which Mr. Crandall's birds of paradise were captured, but the majority of the many thousands of softbills imported annually into the British Isles, Europe and North America are trapped with more commercially successful methods. Due to the heavy losses frequently suffered by both the trapper and exporter, the number caught is probably several times greater than the number finally retailed to aviculturists and zoological gardens. In some countries itinerant middlemen may purchase the birds from the trappers and in turn resell them to exporters based in the cities.

Native trappers are often supplied with, or own, mist nets, and with these are able to greatly increase their daily catch, with less risk of injury to the birds. The tree-top dwelling species which seldom venture below the forest canopy, which can be almost two hundred feet above the ground in some tropical rain forests, are naturally the most difficult to obtain. The trapping of these birds, which is best attempted around fruiting or flowering trees, involves using ladders, poles and pulleys, and much strenuous climbing. For the low dwelling species mist nets are practically infallible. If set at random in forested areas they cannot fail to trap birds in time, whereas if the location is chosen with care after studying bird movements the results can be startling. Particularly good places for hanging these nets are around fruiting and flowering trees, across flight paths leading to these trees or to drinking places, across a gap in a forested ridge which gives birds access to an adjoining valley, and between patches of cover in wooded grassland or secondary growth.

Mist nets are made of very strong nylon thread, and are available in various mesh sizes, lengths and heights. They are normally hung between two poles or telescoping rods, and from the front are virtually invisible. Several thicker horizontal lines run across the length of the net, and birds flying forcefully into it hang down in pockets of netting over these lines. The smallest size mist nets have half inch square mesh and are suitable for all the smaller softbills, with the exception of a few species of hummingbirds, which barely falter when flying through the mesh.

Several other types of nets are used by trappers, but none as extensively as mist nets. The bat or folding net is designed for netting at night, when roosting birds are driven out of low trees and bushes by the trapper's assistant into the net held on the other side. As the birds enter this oblong piece of netting, secured by the long sides to the tops of two poles, the operator brings the poles together and encloses them.

The clapnet is designed to operate with a pull string after the birds have been attracted with bait or decoys to an area at the side of the net. It is useful for acquiring the ground feeding species of softbills such as starlings, grackles, pittas and thrushes. Spring net traps are similar but are generally automatic. They are available commercially and have a rigid wire frame which folds back to form a half circle when set, with the bottom half secured firmly to the ground with small stakes. In the centre of the straight side is a bait dish into which fits the release arm. When the dish is depressed the powerful spring brings the top half over on to the bird. This type of trap is also emminently suitable for ground dwelling species, particularly the insectivorous ones, but only where ants do not abound. In most equatorial rain forests the use of live insect bait is impractical as the struggling insects are easy prey for the innumerable ants which seem to frequent every tree and every square yard of jungle. Without insects to attract the birds these traps are useless of course.

Birds often arrive from India with feathers missing from the breast and wings, and this is frequently where they have been caught with bird lime and had the feathers removed, although it is possible to remove the gum with various oils. The method of producing bird lime varies from country to country, but is based mainly upon the sap of resinous trees, particularly the latex of ficus species. The favourite method of the Indian bird trapper is to use a long pole which has been smeared with bird lime at the end. The pole is often made up of several sections of bamboo fitted together like a fishing rod, and the trapper lies under a tree frequented by the birds he is seeking, or else attracts them by using a live owl decoy, and slowly pushes his pole up through the branches. Segments are added until the gum-smeared tip is within reach of the bird, which is then quickly and expertly touched with the pole. Small birds remain gummed and helpless to the pole, but the larger species fall to the ground as they are unable to use their wings. The lime is normally removed with a vegetable oil and the birds are placed in a cloth bag until the trapper is satisfied with his efforts and returns home.

For smaller softbills, especially the nectar feeders, small twigs are smeared with bird lime and are loosely placed in strategic positions under flowers or fruit likely to attract the birds. When they land upon these conveniently sited perches they become attached by their feet and tumble to the ground. The availability of bird lime offers the trapper almost unlimited possibilities for acquiring birds, as it is only necessary for them to visit a particular place regularly to become vulnerable. Nest sites, roosting sites, display grounds and drinking places are all favourite areas for the birdlimer, and his methods can be as ingenious as his mind can create. Even caged callbirds have been used to entice others, seeking a mate or wanting to attack this intruder to their territory, to land upon the limed perches so conveniently provided above the cage.

Trap cages are seldom used nowadays although the Chardonneret type still has its admirers. Unless incorporated with a call cage this form of trap must be baited with the appropriate food. Half of the top of the cage is hinged to pivot upwards against the tension of a piece of strong elastic, and is held in that position by a thin piece of wood fixed to the centre of the trap door and slotted into a loose perch. This dislodges when a bird alights on it and the door closes.

A common practice, but only where the larger species of softbills are concerned, is to tie the fledgelings feet to a branch beneath the nest, which ensures that the youngsters are reared to nest-leaving age and sometimes beyond, yet are still available when the collector returns. Other birds may be taken from the nest for hand-rearing, and by this means many otherwise unobtainable species become available to the aviculturist. This applies mainly to the hawking birds such as bee-eaters, jacamars and some of the kingfishers, as only the most expert bird trapper would attempt to establish wild caught adult birds. The late Cecil Webb in his book *A Wanderer in the Wind* relates such an occasion in his long collecting career, when a pair of blue-necked bee-eaters were followed to their nest hole in an Indian river bank, and were trapped when leaving the hole early the following morning.

It is often easier to obtain nestlings of some of the larger softbills than it is to trap the adults, which accounts for the many immature cocks of the rock, hornbills and toucans that are offered by the dealers. In South America it is frequently necessary to fell a whole tree to get young toucans from the nest, as these are usually very high in trees devoid of limbs until they reach the forest canopy. Climbing to these nests is therefore a difficult and dangerous undertaking, and the nestlings may well be several feet down inside a natural cavity or old wood-peckers hole. The felling of a tree to obtain young birds requires a great deal of skill so that the area of the trunk where the nest hole is situated is not shattered by the impact. Adjoining trees are often used to cushion the fall. The Amerindian hunters also need to determine the age of the nestlings to ensure that handrearing is a relatively easy task. Unlike their counterparts in Asia, who determine the age of young hornbills from the growth of seeds at the foot of their tree, the South American natives cannot employ this method as the toucans carry their nestlings faecal sacs some distance from the nest site as a safety measure. As well as toucans the Amerindians are adept at handrearing many other birds, and take cocks of the rock from their rock ledge nest sites, and many small fruit-eating birds such as tanagers and hangnests for handrearing, after which they are kept in small woven baskets hanging under the eaves of their huts.

Establishing Softbilled Birds

The establishment of a wild bird to captive conditions is the most crucial period of its life, and yet it is often the time when insufficient care and attention are given to its requirements. Although it must be the duty of the first person concerned with the wild bird—the trapper—to accustom newly caught specimens to captivity, in many cases they are merely supplying an exporter and birds are seldom in their hands long enough for this to be done. The onus therefore falls upon the exporters.

It should be remembered that the capture of a bird and the following succession of events, until such time as it is properly established, are a deviation from its normal routine and therefore place considerable stress upon it. The complete changes of diet, the change of environment, the inhibition of its flight reflexes, and the relative lack of exercise are all stress factors which can seriously affect the health of a bird. The act of establishing a bird quickly and properly plays an important part in its health and longevity in captivity, and entails basically the change-over from natural foods to replacement diets, and the reduction of flight reflexes to such an extent that they are no longer a major force in the bird's behaviour. In short achieving a degree of tameness.

Ideally the full acceptance of captive conditions should have taken place in the exporter's hands, before birds are exposed to the additional strain placed on them by a long air journey and then completely different climatic conditions, but this is seldom the case. Frequently birds are not transferred to a sufficiently varied replacement diet, and are shipped after receiving foods nutritionally different in many respects.

Insectivorous species are often sent off on a diet of maggots and mealworms only, and occasionally on such insects as locusts and grasshoppers which are native to their habitat. Fruit-eating birds are usually accompanied by banana or the harder, longer lasting plantain, and from their condition on arrival it is quite obvious that this has been their sole food item since they were caught. But we must blame the advent of air travel for this, as it is now possible to ship delicate birds within a day or two of their capture, thus ensuring that they arrive alive, even if they remain alive only for a few days after their receipt.

It is I suppose too much to expect exporters to moult out their birds before shipping them, and possibly this is unnecessary anyway, but at least this would be an indication that the birds were fully established and therefore more able to withstand the strain of a long air journey, which in turn would benefit both the consignor and the importer, and the image of aviculture too. Birds should certainly not be shipped when they are moulting, a frequent failing amongst exporters.

In addition to being sent before they are established many stress factors face birds during shipment and on arrival at their destination, and these must be borne in mind and steps taken to counteract them when the birds are received. To reduce the cost of air freight birds are often overcrowded in their shipping crates, although this is a more frequent occurrence in shipments of finches than softbills. Under these conditions there is often a high incidence of infections of the digestive tract. We frequently hear of instances of wrong feeding en route, and occasionally of cases of bad handling, lack of urgency and delays, due of course to lack of knowledge, yet damaging just the same.

Birds shipped too soon after capture and therefore not allowed to regain their pre-capture condition, are unlikely to feed sufficiently during the journey, and are therefore susceptible to infections and changes of temperature due to their lowered resistance. When received by the importer they are subjected to another change of environment and food, and again when they are retailed their food and environment changes. Sometimes a middleman is involved between these transactions, which adds further to the stress placed upon the birds. In one respect only is it fortunate that the factors already considered result in an undernourished bird, as there is less likelihood of death occurring from heart failure.

It is frequently necessary for practically the whole process of establishment or re-establishment of birds to commence when they finally reach the aviculturist or zoo. The first step with most tropical species is to provide them with a temperature of about 75°F (24°C), but it is important that this is associated with fresh air. Reduction from this to a more practical temperature will depend upon the temperature of the quarters in which they will eventually be housed. Within reason the detailed examination of birds for parasites, the washing of beaks, feet and legs and the bathing of eyes should be left for a few days and not carried out immediately upon arrival. This does not apply of course if dirty vents, clogged nostrils and massive infestations of external parasites need immediate attention, or if the birds are to be released into a large cage where subsequent netting would be too distressing. The housing of new arrivals in groups in large cages is not advisable however, and small cages containing a few birds is the best arrangement for the first week, as their feeding and treatment is easier to control, catching them is far easier and less distressing and a watchful eye can be kept with more accuracy. As a general rule an antibiotic could be administered for the first four days to reduce the possibility of a flare-up of bacteria, normally present in the gut, which can become pathogenic when a bird's condition is lowered. Administration of antibiotics for longer periods could do irreparable harm in reducing symbiotic bacteria to a dangerously low level. The water offered should be tepid and certainly not taken straight from the cold tap, not only from the drinking point of view but in case it is used for bathing.

A glucose or nectar solution can be offered to debiltated specimens as they will derive much benefit from the energy quickly released from easily assimilated foods. It may be necessary to assist birds by dipping their beaks into the liquid until they appreciate how palatable it is. A tonic could also be added to stimulate the general food intake.

The lights in the birdroom where newly imported specimens are kept should be left on at night for the first week to encourage feeding during the late evening and early morning when they are completely undisturbed, but the reduction of a wild bird's flight reflexes is usually a slow business. Movement in the birdroom should be slower and more deliberate than is normal when dealing with birds. For the first few days they should be left alone to rest and feed for as long as possible each day without being disturbed, unless their condition requires a close watch to be kept on ailing or non-feeding specimens. Even this should be done from a distance if possible, as it is upsetting to birds to be stared at from close range. If they are housed in cages which have to be entered for servicing, they should always be allowed an escape route away from the corners of the cage or flight or they will panic in their attempts to remain at a safe distance. Only when they have settled down should they be exposed to movement, voices and closer scrutiny.

The acceptance of captive diets is easier to achieve in the case of the fruit-eating species than with the insectivorous ones. Also there are few omnivorous softbills that could be considered difficult to transfer to captive diets, and of these several species of manakins are probably the most difficult. They would not reach these shores however unless they were reasonably well established and accepting a diet of mixed fruit and possibly mealworms, and the aviculturist fortunate to obtain them has merely to make them accept a more satisfactory diet.

The truly insectivorous species are the most backward in accepting captive diets, and the process of getting them to eat replacement foods is commonly known as "meating-off". Occasionally these birds are accustomed to accepting inanimate foods prior to shipment, or if not can soon be tempted onto more sustaining foods by an experienced aviculturist. Others are more challenging, particularly the hawking bee-eaters and some flycatchers, which are often restricted to a diet of maggots and mealworms until they succumb to malnutrition. Meating-off should not commence as soon as a bird is captured, or, if it is shipped as soon as the exporter receives it, immediately it arrives at its final destination. For several days it should be allowed to settle down and feed solely upon live food if it wishes, even if only maggots and mealworms are available. After this the process of changing over to a more satisfactory diet can commence. Many methods have been used to achieve this, but the most successful are as follows: For the larger insectivorous species such as the rollers and motmots the beak should be tapped with a strip of meat or a ball of minced meat on a piece of wire until the bird snaps at it, even if only out of annoyance. After several days they should have recognised the meat as a palatable food and will commence to accept it out of feeding dishes. It is often possible to prise open a birds beak and place food items just inside, allowing them to swallow these in their own time. Force-feeding (forcing food right down the gullet) should never be attempted with the softbills.

The most successful method of meating-off the smaller species of insectivorous birds is to mix their live food with an insectile mixture or minced meat. A little honey can be added to improve the chances of the mixture adhering to the live food. Maggots serve this purpose fairly well, being adapted for existence in a semi-fluid material, but mealworms do not live long after being coated with honey, and are therefore of little use as they are not so readily accepted. Several other methods of meating-off have been used, one of the most successful being the introduction of an established bird of the same or allied species with the same feeding habits, the new birds quickly learning by example. A darkened box, with a small hole cut in the top to allow a pinpoint of light to draw attention to the feeding dish has also been used, although mainly by trappers enticing a newly caught bird to feed, as opposed to meating-off one which will at least accept live food.

Toucan Barbet. Like all the larger Barbets this attractive South American bird cannot be trusted where smaller species or breeding birds are concerned.

low, Blue-winged Pitta. The Pittas must be kept on an earth floor and provided with logs and rocks to perch on. Although otherwise terrestrial, they roost in trees.

Silver-throated Tanager. An inexpensive hardy bird which can safely be wintered out onc
acclimatised. A common species, in the wild and in captivity, it is always popular because of i
attractive colour scheme.

Below: Red-fronted Barbet. An inoffensive East African Barbet which is easy to maintain i
provided with thick semi-rotten tree trunks. It can be kept with a collection of small softbil
with impunity.

Acclimatisation

The acclimatisation and establishment of tropical birds are of course connected, as it follows that unless a bird is well established to captive conditions it is hardly likely to become thoroughly accustomed to completely different climatic conditions. On the other hand birds housed indoors in heated conservatory aviaries and birdrooms can be well established, yet still not be acclimatised.

The definition of acclimatise is "to accustom to a new climate", which of course includes all atmospheric conditions, not just temperature. Whatever the definition of the word however, the fact remains that to be completely acclimatised to temperate weather conditions tropical birds must be accustomed to, and therefore able to withstand, the changes in humidity, dampness, reduction in temperature, frequent sudden changes in air movement during the winter months and a reduction in the number of hours of daylight available for feeding.

The acclimatisation of exotic softbills can only begin during the summer months, and the only practical way of doing this is to simulate, when the birds are received from the tropics, the high daytime temperatures they have been accustomed to, with a slight reduction at night if possible. This temperature, about 75°F (24°C), can then be reduced slowly over a period of perhaps three weeks, until the use of artificial heat can be discontinued. By this time the temperature indoors will be very similar to that outside, and the birds can then be allowed access to the outdoors on warm, calm days, but should still be shut in at night to prevent them being exposed to rain or cold winds while roosting. The time spent outdoors should then be increased until all summer weather conditions are experienced.

Many softbills can be acclimatised relatively quickly and can be given access to outdoor flights during their first winter in the country provided they were imported early in the year, and were therefore able to spend most of the summer out of doors. Because of the vagaries of temperate winters however, it is always advisable to provide heated shelters for birds that are wintered out. While they can adapt to cold, dry conditions, the damp, misty coldness experienced on many winter days can be very treacherous, particularly if the winter food intake is not up to standard.

The temperature in their outdoor shelters need not be high, as extremes would then be created when the outside temperature dropped below freezing point, making the birds less resistant to the cold when they went outside. A temperature of about 45°F (7·2°C) is sufficient, and is not too warm to cause extremes. When birds make use of their shelter during winter nights the conditions created are the reverse of the higher day than night temperatures encountered in the natural state. It is unlikely that this has an adverse effect upon the birds health however, for as far as we know the only birds to have a daily cycle of torpidity are the hummingbirds, and they become torpid during the hours of darkness whatever the temperature. Other species, which sleep as opposed to becoming torpid, would not use as many food calories to maintain their body temperature due to the higher air temperature, a fact which should be taken into account when providing the correct winter diet.

Although the outdoor shelter temperature and the above remarks concerning wintering out apply to the hardier species of softbills such as the thrushes, starlings, jays, tree pies, orioles, hornbills and toucans, all of which are well able to acclimatise completely to temperate conditions without any heat providing they are kept in sheltered positions, they certainly do not apply to the terrestrial tropical softbills. These—the pittas, quail doves, bushchats etc.—and the fleshy-legged fruit pigeons, would almost certainly suffer from frostbite if kept out of doors during below-zero temperatures. These birds must be kept indoors and provided with gentle artificial heat. This also applies to the smaller species of tanagers, and to the cotingas, manakins, bee-eaters and flowerpeckers. It is quite possible that many of these and other so-called delicate birds could withstand winter conditions equally as well as the hardier species if provided with the correct diet, but few owners are prepared to take such risks, whatever the odds, with specimens that are irreplacable.

The acclimatisation of any tropical birds should not be attempted until the provision of a suitable diet has been carefully investigated, as birds suffering from a deficiency of energy food nutrients stand little chance of surviving a harsh winter, or at least will be severely debilitated when spring arrives. Softbills have a body temperature of about 105°F (40·6°C), and this usually drops two degrees when they are roosting. When the air temperature drops they must produce more heat from the metabolisation of energy foods to counteract any possible loss of body heat, and in addition must provide sufficient energy to maintain their physiological functions, particularly during the time of day when they are most active. It is therefore wrong to feed a bird being wintered out upon the same diet as birds housed indoors in "summer" conditions. The energy food content of the diet must be increased; and for omnivorous and insectivorous birds this can be done by replacing some of the honey used for moistenting their insectile mixture with corn oil or animal fat, which have a higher calorific content. Increasing the soya flour or sweet biscuit meal in the mixture, or providing more mealworms will give a similar result. It must also be remembered that birds wintered out have reduced feeding time unless lighting is provided in their shelters, so their food must be available immediately it becomes light.

In order that sufficient protein is ingested when the feeding time and therefore the total food intake is reduced during the winter, the protein content of the diet should also be increased. If additional mealworms or soya flour are used to provide the extra carbohydrate these will also supply the protein. If, however, animal or vegetable oils are used then protein rich foods such as meat or fish meal or raw minced beef should be added to the mixture. These increases must be tailed off as spring approaches and the environmental temperature increases, otherwise fat will be deposited as less energy is needed to maintain the body temperature, and the birds will be unfit for breeding until too late in the summer. To reduce the risk of respiratory infections the vitamin D content of the diet should also be increased.

In temperate regions acclimatisation in reverse to what is considered normal is occasionally necessary. The high altitude tropical species of softbills, which include such prized possessions as the quetzal, the mountain tanagers and toucans and those birds of paradise which inhabit the mountain ranges of New Guinea are often pampered in captivity, and provided with conditions more suited to their lowland relatives. Birds from high altitudes, particularly those of the New World, as a rule do not thrive in enclosed conservatory aviaries, where hot and rather humid conditions persist. The quetzal, a native of the cloud forests of Central America is a typical example. Found up to 9,600 ft. above sea level it is accustomed to damp and cool temperatures approximately 30 degrees below those of the coastal lowlands, on the basis that the air temperature drops one degreee for every 300 ft. ascended. This also applies to the mountain tanagers and high altitude hummingbirds, which presented bird collectors with many problems in the days before regular air services made it possible to ship them direct from Bogota and Quito, both high in the Andes. Before this is was necessary to transport them down the western slope of the Andes to the humid lowlands and the port of embarkation, where the extreme climatic conditions resulted in many losses.

Housing

In temperate climates where cold, damp conditions persist for long periods during the winter months, the housing of tropical softbills outside throughout the year is not as risky as is often thought provided that the necessary precautions are taken. The need for tropical lowland species to have been gradually accustomed to outdoor temperatures before being wintered out has already been emphasised, plus their additional food requirements. There remains the question of accommodation, which will provide ample space for exercise and shelter from rain, winds and draughts.

There is little point in dwelling upon the size and shape of aviaries as these can be as varied as imagination and circumstances allow. If artificial light is not provided in the shelters it should be remembered that the reduction of exercise resulting from less daylight hours will not offset the increased energy requirements needed to combat the lower temperatures, and therefore it is advisable to provide mild heat for even the hardiest species. The shelters must be completely enclosed of course, with access through a small entrance hole only.

The aspect of aviaries is important. They should always be sited to back the prevailing winds although heavy gauge polythene sheeting is excellent for covering aviaries in exposed positions, or for using as a windbreak. When heat is provided in the shelters it is necessary to insulate to prevent undue loss of warmth, and the roof is the most effective area for insulating of course, if possible with a false ceiling. To prevent draughts from blowing directly into the shelter a baffle should be fitted inside the entrance, but must be far enough back from the opening or

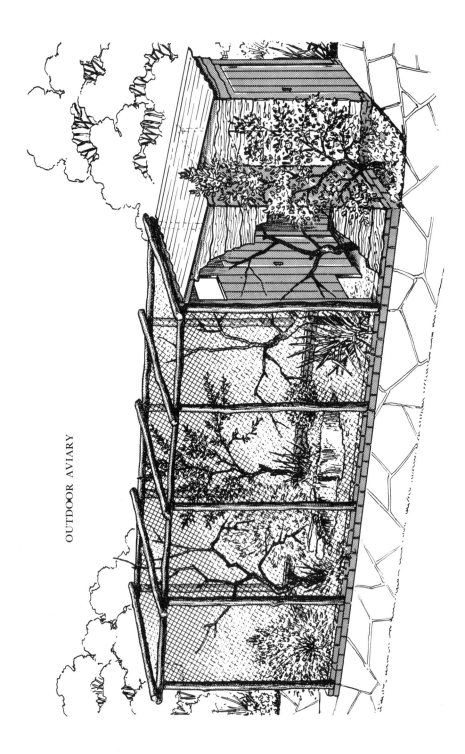

OUTDOOR AVIARY

the birds will be deterred from using it. If a window is to be included in the roof area of the shelter it should be remembered that although sunlight is beneficial to birds, direct rays through glass from which there is no escape will cause death.

Chicken mesh is suitable for softbill flights, but its length of life, particularly in industrial areas, is rather short, and the plastic covered mesh is well worth the extra expense. Square, welded mesh is by far the easiest to handle and is also available galvanised or with a plastic finish.

To provide nesting sites, seclusion and a choice of perching, aviaries should be planted with resilient trees and shrubs, and the dense growth of privet species is emminently suitable for the smaller softbills. For additional perching space and for roosting during fine weather, dead branches should be so positioned that they reach the top of the flight.

Indoor accommodation for softbilled birds ranges from the small cages and indoor flights of the aviculturist and some zoological gardens still, where the cage fronts are wired, and sawdust, sand or paper covers the floor; to the large modern bird exhibits where glass is used with great effect and the compartments are landscaped and planted. It is generally accepted that the size of a bird cage is dependent upon the size of the birds to be kept, and that their length should be approximately six times that of the bird, by four lengths high and three lengths deep. The perches should vary in thickness and are best placed at either end of the cage, allowing space for turning between the perch and the end of the cage, while allowing the maximum flying space from perch to perch.

From the presentation point of view the conservatory aviary principle of housing exotic softbills cannot be improved upon, and they are of course the most suited of all avicultural subjects for maintaining in planted aviaries as many do not destroy the vegetation. Two basic types of exhibit are usually incorporated in modern bird houses. First there is the walk-through or free-flight aviary, where restraint is achieved by using bead curtains or by darkening the entrance and exit porches. These exhibits can become lush botanical collections housing a few nectar

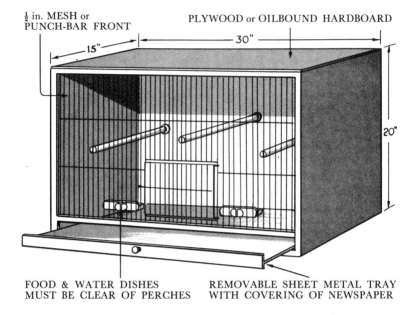

½ in. MESH or
PUNCH-BAR FRONT   PLYWOOD or OILBOUND HARDBOARD

15"

30"

20"

FOOD & WATER DISHES   REMOVABLE SHEET METAL TRAY
MUST BE CLEAR OF PERCHES   WITH COVERING OF NEWSPAPER

INDOOR CAGE. ABSOLUTE MINIMUM SIZE FOR A PAIR OF SMALL
TANAGERS, HONEYCREEPERS, WHITE EYES, ETC.

feeders and other inoffensive species, as far as the plants are
concerned, or more impressive avicultural displays containing
the larger softbills. The latter are more difficult to achieve
because of the destructive nature of many of the larger species.
The second type of exhibit in conservatory aviaries is the glass
fronted compartment. These vary in size from the small
"jewel" cages to the very much larger ones which are ideal for
mixed groups of birds. Although there is more daily work
involved in the maintenance of planted exhibits, it could never
be argued that the construction of these costly methods of
housing birds is not worth the expense. If we are to continue
to maintain the rarer species of softbills in both public and
privately owned collections it is surely beyond criticism to
endeavour to create the finest conditions possible.

The basic ingredient of the planted bird house is of course the soil, which can be sterilised, but unless the droppings of every new bird are subjected to the most stringent microscopical examination, and the daily sterilisation of footwear and equipment is carried out, there is little point in taking this precaution. One of the best mixtures for growing tropical plants comprises equal parts of good loam soil, peat and sharp sand. The loam should not be taken from land on which poultry have been kept as this may be contaminated. This soil mixture, moistened, has proved suitable for pittas and other terrestrial species, keeping their feet in excellent condition.

When birds and plants are kept together the birds must be chosen with great care, as a number of the softbills are very destructive. Destructiveness is associated with the size of the birds, the size of the area in which they are to be housed, and the type of plants used. In a large well established planted compartment it would be possible to keep a pair of small, fairly destructive species such as the black-spotted barbet, as the shoots and leaves destroyed on each plant would not seriously affect their growth. If the same birds were allowed to concentrate their efforts upon one or two small plants these would naturally soon be destroyed as their buds would be nipped off as soon as they appeared. On the other hand if their quarters contained only kentia and phoenix palms the barbet's attentions would have little effect. American oropendolas however are adept at weaving together even the toughest palm fronds while they are still growing. Other very destructive softbills are the orioles, tree pies, Buffons and Knysna touracos, tits, yuhinas, zosterops and most species of tanagers. The aracaries are perhaps the most destructive of all, particularly to low growing plants. Fortunately the choice species which are so desirable for housing in conservatory aviaries are eminently suitable also. The manakins, kingfishers, bee-eaters, cotingas, motmots, pittas and wood hoopoes for instance are non-destructive, as are also the rollers, fruit pigeons, wagtails and surprisingly the red-crested and white-headed touracos.

Although the growth of plants is mainly dependent upon the

wise choice of birds therefore, there are certain plants which are more able to withstand the attentions of destructive birds. Generally speaking they are the plants with large leaves, and consequently large shoots like many of the ficus species. Also the plants which have very tough fibrous leaves such as the palms already mentioned, and the low growing dracaenas; and trees with fine leaves and branches such as grevillea, which do not afford perching spaces for the larger birds.

The humidity is essentially quite high because of the presence of pools, waterfalls and the moist nature of the soil in conservatory aviaries, caused by the frequent watering necessary for the plant life. This is increased by the daily routine of sponging droppings from the leaves, and scrubbing the rocks and dead branches provided for perching. To encourage plant growth the temperature must be kept between 60° and 70°F (15·6° and 21°C), although the overhead windows, providing the daylight essential for plant growth, will cause a rapid increase in temperature on sunny days due to solar heat gain. Sufficient ventilation, without causing draughts, is of the utmost importance to avoid excessive temperature increases on very hot days, but the heat and humidity characteristic of the conservatory does not appear to inconvenience the tropical softbills of lowland origin, provided of course that they are not over fat.

Although the top layer of soil should be replaced every few months, the main disadvantage of housing birds over soil is the risk of infection due to the difficulty of removing all droppings and scattered food particles daily. In this respect only are the concrete floors of the old type bird houses more hygenic as they can be scrubbed and disinfected frequently. In addition to decomposing food encouraging the growth of pathogenic organisms, there is also the danger of an infected bird passing on parasitic and bacterial infections.

The use of glass instead of mesh to restrain birds has much in its favour in addition to providing an uninterrupted view of both plant and bird life. It allows the feeding of a wide variety of live food including crickets, blowflies and locusts, as there is little chance of them escaping if all opening windows are covered with gauze. Glass completely cancels the risk of draughts and in collections open to the public deters feeding and teasing. It is possible to control temperature and humidity more effectively, and the isolation and treatment of infections can be more efficiently carried out.

Initially the risk of birds flying into the glass and injuring themselves is fairly high, but until they have become accustomed to it and accept it as a barrier it should be whitewashed. This can be removed gradually after several days. The risk of birds flying into the glass when alarmed is always present of course.

Nutrition

The science of bird feeding is a new one, as indeed is that of wild animal nutrition as a whole, and as the subject is relatively little known hard and fast rules cannot really be laid down upon the best feeding methods to adopt. Generally speaking it is known that the higher vertebrates require the basic food components, which are protein, fat, carbohydrate, vitamins, mineral salts and water or moisture derived from their food. It is also known that malnutrition is the greatest cause of death of captive wild animals. This does not necessarily mean insufficient food however, but rather a poorly balanced diet where the proportion of food components was incorrect and did not constitute a complete ration.

From what is known of softbill diets it is still unwise to state emphatically that a particular diet may be correct or sufficient merely because a particular species has bred successfully as a result of its use. This is where the art of animal husbandry plays such an important part in bird keeping, otherwise every person feeding this diet to a compatible pair of the same species of bird would theoretically achieve the same results, which is often far from the case. Therefore, although the nutrition of softbills must be considered the most important aspect of their maintenance, housing, temperature and acclimatisation must be taken into consideration also, as they are all so closely connected.

Lacking the detailed scientific data available on the nutritional requirements of domestic breeds of birds, for their wild ancestors we can only arrive at a reasonably satisfactory diet by comparing the feeding methods which have produced favourable results with what is known of the natural diet of wild birds, and apply to this the known requirements of domestic poultry. Although the domestic hen is basically the same creature, with the same body functions and a similar digestive system, it would of course be foolish to advocate a diet for wild birds based solely upon the requirements of a bird bred specifically for the production of meat and eggs. However, the knowledge of their vitamin and mineral salt requirements, of the protein necessary for feather production and carbohydrate needed to produce body heat, can be of great assistance. It is then that the specialised feeding habits of the wild bird in its natural state must be taken into consideration, as it is only from this knowledge that their varied requirements of protein and energy foods can be ascertained. For instance it is known that the combinations of great activity, high temperature and relatively large surface area require a high intake of carbohydrates or fats, and on this basis we might be forgiven for believing that the sunbird's requirements would basically be the same as that of the hummingbird. But, from the studies of the wild bird's food preferences, plus the success of certain captive diets, it is obvious that the hummingbird requires a far higher carbohydrate intake than not only the sunbird but all other softbills.

Although there is no doubt therefore that softbill diets must contain the following food constituents, in most instances the balancing of these in the correct proportions is still a matter for conjecture.

Protein
Protein is necessary for building muscle in young birds, and in adult life is required as a maintenance food for replacing cells and tissues. It cannot be classed as an energy food in the same sense as the fats and carbohydrates even though it contains approximately the same calories per gm. (4) as carbohydrate. It is basically a body building food and is only used to provide energy when the fat and carbohydrate intake is insufficient to do this, or when the protein intake is very excessive. Feathers are practically pure protein, and eggs contain a high percentage.

Crude Fibre

This is basically the structural component of plants, where it is known as cellulose, but its carbohydrate content is unavailable to most birds as they lack the enzymes necessary to break it down. The fibre in the meals of animal origin used in bird foods is partly digestible as it contains protein. The higher the cellulose content of a bird food the lower is its digestibility, as birds are not equipped to deal with this as are certain mammals, in which the gut bacteria assist in its breakdown. Fibre-rich plant products such as rolled oats and ground barley can be used to reduce the nutritional value of a food mixture.

Carbohydrates

These are the main energy producing nutrients and are sub-divided into the monosaccharides and the disaccharides, which are the sugars; and the polysaccharides or starches, of both plant and animal origin. They are known as the nitrogen-free extractives, and the percentage present in a food is often quoted as N.F.E. In addition to supplying the energy needed for the body functions carbohydrates also assist in the utilisation of body fats. The provision of sugars and starches in bird diets fortunately usually exceeds the percentage of fats or oils.

Fats and Oils

As birds are warm blooded creatures they must be provided with sufficient energy foods to maintain their body temperature by replacing heat loss. In addition, the body functions of blood circulation and respiration require muscular action powered by energy. A gm. of fat or oil produces approximately nine calories of energy, more than double that of proteins or carbohydrates. The intake of energy sources obviously must be carefully regulated, and must be related to such factors as the air temperature at which the birds are kept, and to a lesser extent the availability of ample exercise space. Although a fatty deposit under the skin, acting as insulation because of its non-conductor capacity, is essential to birds wintered out without heat, it would be disastrous for birds kept under normal conditions. The number of calories in a diet is known as the metabolisable energy content, and is usually given in terms of calories per lb. of food. Where possible the calorie content of the softbill diets given in appendix B will be expressed as calories per lb. Food mixtures containing a high calorific content should be fed in moderation.

Minerals and trace elements

The major mineral elements (calcium, phosphorus, potassium, sodium, sulphur, chlorine, iron and magnesium) are required by animals in greater supply that are the minor or trace elements (iodine, zinc, copper etc.), and the composition of commercially available mixtures is graded accordingly. They are essential for bone growth, for the production of egg shell, for assisting in the conversion of vegetable protein into flesh, and for the production of red blood cells. The mineral content is very low in items used in bird feeding with the exception of meat and bone and fish meals. It is therefore essential that a mineral salt and trace element supplement should be included in the diet to counteract this deficiency.

Vitamins

From the requirements of poultry it is known that birds need the same vitamins as mammals, with the possible exception of vitamin C, which like most mammals they can probably synthesise. Vitamins are of great importance and without them it is impossible to keep birds in good health. The vitamins assist in the production of bone, are essential for the metabolism of fats and carbohydrates, and are necessary for correct nerve functioning, amongst other things. The ailments resulting from vitamin and mineral salt deficiences are discussed in detail in chapter 8.

Water or moisture

All foodstuffs contain a percentage of water, and this varies from as much as 80% in fruits and vegetables to 10% in seeds and beans. Imago insects are approximately half moisture,

Abyssinian Ground Thrush. A rare East African species which is less terrestrial than the common-y available Asiatic ground Thrushes.

Below, Van den Bock's Pitta. A rare bird from South East Asia, this beautiful Pitta has been ncreasingly available to aviculture recently.

Spotted Morning Warbler. Actually a relative of the Thrushes, not the Warblers, this specie
has been exported from East Africa on several occasions in recent years. They are highly insect
vorous and completely inoffensive to other birds.

while the larval stages contain much more. The blowfly larvae and the mealworm have a moisture content of about 70%. It is not really surprising therefore that the bee-eaters, which are not known to drink, and some species of flycatchers which seldom drink, can derive sufficient moisture from an insect diet. All other softbills require drinking water in addition to the moisture they derive from their food. It is well known that birds cannot perspire, and any loss of heat must occur through naked or sparsely feathered areas of the body, or through panting. Consequently there is not the loss of water that there would be from sweating, but a certain amount is lost through defecation. The presence of water in the diet is essential for the absorption of digestible food components and therefore for life. The water content of the hummingbird's liquid diet provides sufficient to sustain life, probably more than enough, if as we are led to believe, some hummingbirds are more insectivorous than nectivorous in their natural state.

Due to the wide range of foods taken by softbilled birds in the wild state, it follows that their feeding in captivity will be of a more complex nature than for most other groups of birds. It can be simplified however, while not allowing simplicity to interfere with sufficiency, by dividing these birds into five groups, for which separate diets can be formulated. Allowances can then be made for the more specialised forms within each group.

As the natural diet of a bird forms the basis of its diet in aviculture, it is obvious that this must be used as the sole criterion when classifying softbills in this manner, with the exception of the nectivorous birds. For the latter the intake of nectar, insects and fruit in the wild is still insufficiently known to be able to place a percentage tag upon their food intake, and some even have a seasonal variation of diet. Neither is it possible to provide sufficient insects for the more insectivorous species of hummingbirds and sunbirds, and they are often confined to a liquid diet, with perhaps a negligible number of drosophila daily. Therefore the only satisfactory method of classifying these birds from the feeding point of view is to base this upon the captive feeding methods which have proved successful.

It must be appreciated however that while these groupings form the basis of softbill nutrition, captive conditions often create artificial behaviour where feeding is concerned. This is frequently so in mixed collections, where a wider variety of foods is available to all the birds. Unusual and unexpected foods are occasionally taken, but these are often due to individual variations rather than to an avicultural group as a whole. More frequently, however, these so-called abnormal feeding habits are really providing a diet more akin to the birds natural foods, than being merely a captive influenced variation. When such preferences become apparent efforts should be made to obtain information upon the bird's natural diet to ascertain if the regular intake of unusual foods could be harmful. For example chloropsis in community aviaries have greedily eaten fresh shrimps provided for kingfishers, but shrimps are very similar in appearance to the orthopterous insects which figure largely in the natural diet of these birds and are not harmful if fed in moderation, but an excessive intake would probably result in diarrhoea. Sunbitterns, normally fed on minced meat, live food and insectile mixture also relish shrimps and small fish such as whitebait, which are more in keeping with their natural intake as they feed along shallow water courses upon aquatic life.

In all instances the diets suggested in succeeding pages are based upon the requirements of birds housed under normal conditions. This means being kept out of doors during the summer months, and brought inside and provided with mild heat during the winter, plus of course reasonable exercise space. The more exacting requirements of birds wintered out, of breeding birds, of birds being established or acclimatised, and the reduced requirements of birds housed indoors all year round are discussed in the relevant chapters. From the nutritional point of view softbilled birds can be sub-divided into five groups —the nectivorous, insectivorous, frugivorous, omnivorous and carnivorous softbills. A more detailed examination of these classifications is given in Part II.

The Nectivorous Softbills

This group includes all softbilled birds whose natural diet includes a large proportion of nectar taken from the calyxes of flowers. The percentage of nectar imbibed varies considerably among the species in this group, and they demand a wider range of foods in general than any of the other groups.

Although the hummingbirds are known to feed upon both insects and nectar in their natural habitat, which of these predominates is not definite. From the captive aspect it is known that a high intake of carbohydrate is necessary to provide energy for their incessant activity and the highest metabolic rate known. Although it is accepted that insects are necessary to provide protein, if the energy content of the small arthropods and their larvae available to the wild humming bird are similar to that of the insects for which we have records, if insects alone formed the diet there would surely be insufficient calories to sustain such an active bird. Whatever the natural diet, in captivity the hummingbirds thrive on nectar mixtures containing a high percentage of sugars, plus a protein percentage more in keeping with the requirements of other birds. Fruit flies are normally the only form of live food available to hummingbirds and are an important item of their diet. Although theoretically they are unnecessary from the nutritional aspect if ample protein is provided in the nectar, it is unwise to feed any bird on a permanent liquid diet. As well as stimulating interest the provision of bulk in the form of live food must be a necessary item for a digestive system accustomed to it in the wild state.

Many nectar mixtures have been extolled, and it would be pointless and confusing to repeat them as they are so varied in content, although fairly similar in their final analysis. In the early days of hummingbird keeping they were normally given a honey and water solution, and longevity records were quoted in weeks rather than years. While the honey provided the energy requirements it is very low in protein and practically devoid of vitamins, even vitamin B_1 which is necessary for the metabolisation of the carbohydrate. Nowadays it is possible to purchase high protein foods with added vitamins and mineral salts, although the energy content of the diet can still be provided by using sugar. If it is desired to produce a completely home made food many other ingredients can be used. These mainly take the form of an invalid or baby food together with a meat extract and a water soluble form of vitamin concentrate.

As the other species of nectivorous softbills do not need such a massive intake of energy food, hummingbird mixtures are both unnecessary and unsuitable for them. The honeycreepers and sunbirds are less dependent upon nectar than the humming-birds, but it still comprises a large proportion of their captive diet. Although some East African sunbirds are forced to make local migrations in search of flowering vegetation, many vary their diet from nectar to insects according to the season and availability of food. Even the more insectivorous species require 85% of their food intake in the form of nectar, the remainder being insects, mainly drosophila, houseflies, small maggots and mealworms. Several of the honeycreepers, particularly the isthmian and blue species need slightly less nectar and more fruit, whereas the remaining species and the bananaquits and flowerpeckers manage on a diet of half nectar and half fruit and insectile mixture, plus a little live food. The spiderhunters, although basically insect-eaters in the wild, thrive on a similar diet. The fruit which all these birds find in the wild state mainly takes the form of small berries, a fact which should be remembered when dicing their fruit.

Even the sunbirds that feed mainly upon insects in the wild, such as the yellow-backed, ruby-cheeked and collared sunbirds do well on an ad-lib supply of nectar and insects, the nectar of course forming the bulk of their diet. Sunbirds rarely accept fruit although the violet-backed sunbird is a notable exception. As a general rule the shorter beaked species are more insectivorous, this being particularly noticeable in the bananaquit, black-headed honeycreeper and violet-backed sunbird. None of the honeycreepers or the sunbirds require the high energy intake of the hummingbirds, and the insectile mixtures offered should be fairly rich in protein but low in fats and carbohydrates, in view of the amount derived from the liquid portion of their diet. Honey should be used in preference to sugar as it contains less carbohydrate and is richer in mineral salts. All the sunbirds and the more exacting honeycreepers, in which nectar forms the bulk of the food intake, should be given a honey solution fortified with a high protein food and a vitamin supplement. The other honeycreepers and the spiderhunters which are obtaining protein from the insects and insectile mixture provided, do not need such nutritious nectar, and a honey and water solution, with added vitamins, is sufficient.

Nectar mixtures should always be renewed late in the afternoon, when it is common practice to replace more complex mixtures with a honey and water solution, as this is sufficient for the short feeding period left before roosting time, and the following morning before the fresh mixture is provided.

Flowerpeckers show considerable variation of feeding habits. One group, the pardalotes, are basically insectivorous, and the endemic New Guinea species are frugivorous, the remainder favouring berries, nectar and insects, depending upon local availability. Some are well adapted for a diet of berries, mainly the large-seeded mistletoe berries, as they have an alimentary system which allows these easily digested foods to by-pass the stomach and enter the intestine direct from the oesophagous. Insects are digested in the normal manner in the stomach. Studies of their maintenance in captivity indicate that a diet consisting of equal parts of soft fruit and nectar are essential, together with an ad lib supply of drosophila. The nectar mixture should contain more than just honey and water, and one that has proved successful is given in appendix B. The flowerpeckers favour nectar, but should not be allowed continual access to it, as an almost complete liquid diet has led to digestive disturbances. Also, if the mixture is not exactly to their liking, and particularly if it is too weak, they are inclined to feed messily, flicking nectar everywhere, which has caused blocked nostrils.

The South African sugarbirds are seldom available to aviculturists and feed mainly upon the nectar of the protea, and insects. As they have not been observed to feed on any other plants it can only be assumed that protea nectar is of a highly individualistic nature, although possibly in flavour only. Perhaps one day sufficient will be gathered for analysis.

The Frugivorous Softbills

The frugivorous species are the easiest of all the softbills to maintain, but it must be remembered that from the captive point of view there is no such thing as a purely frugivorous bird. No softbill can remain in good condition for long in captivity on a diet of cultivated fruit alone. The analyses given in appendix A prove that the fruits (and vegetables) most frequently offered to the fruit-eating species are nutritionally unsound. The protein content averages only 0·9%, fat is not represented and the total calorie content is approximately 85 calories per 100 gm. of food if sultanas and currants are included, otherwise it is only 40 calories per 100 gm. Vitamin D is absent, and the other vitamins are poorly represented. A moulting bird would have difficulty in replacing its feathers on a diet so low in protein, and whereas the calcium and phosphorus of fruit would probably be sufficient for an adult non-breeding bird, this could not be metabolised anyway due to the absence of vitamin D. It is therefore not surprising that the "more difficult" species of fruit eating birds such as the manakins, cotingas and some of the tanagers, are incapable of withstanding the journey from exporter to retailer as they frequently seem to be offered only a fruit diet before shipment. In actual fact these birds are omnivorous, and in the wild state insects from an appreciable part of their food intake.

There are, however, softbilled birds which are less exacting in their requirements than the omnivorous species mentioned above, and these deserve to be classed as frugivorous softbills, although needing more than just fruit, as already explained. With one exception it is questionable anyway whether any species of bird lives solely upon fruit in the wild state, and although we do not know the composition of the fruit (berries) which are favoured by wild tropical birds, and frequently not even which berries are favoured, it is known that their diet includes shoots and buds, which are rich in protein, and occasionally insects. The fruit pigeons, perhaps the most frugivorous of all, have been observed on several occasions flocking to salt licks and other areas rich in mineral deposits, where the earth has been avidly eaten. In captivity both they and the other frugivorous species, especially the mousebirds, greedily eat maggots and mealworms. An exception to the rule, the oilbird, is known to feed solely upon the nuts of certain palm trees, which have a very high oil content, but are low in protein. These birds provide proof that it is within the capabilities of a species to develop highly specialised feeding habits and maintain their numbers on a diet which would normally be insufficient to support breeding and rearing. They also provide evidence that the fruit pigeons cannot exist solely upon fruit in the wild. Due to the low protein content of its diet the young oilbird spends up to one hundred and twenty days in the nest, becoming very fat, but growing (from the protein point of view the production of flesh and feathers) very slowly. Young fruit pigeons are fed on pigeons milk for the first few days of their lives and gain weight rapidly, and are able to leave the nest at the age of three weeks, almost fully feathered. Pigeons milk is therefore highly nutritious and is obviously rich in protein and could hardly be produced from a diet consisting solely of fruit. Possibly their intake of buds and shoots and even insects increases while they are incubating. The touracos and mousebirds are known to rear their young on insects and therefore cannot be used to add weight to this theory.

The most suitable fruits and vegetables for these birds are bananas, sweet apples, pears, tomatoes, melons, grapes, boiled carrots and sultanas and currants. The latter should be soaked overnight before being used. Bananas, although fairly fattening, have nowhere near the carbohydrate content, and consequently the calories, of sultanas and currants, and it is these which should be fed sparingly. Over-ripe bananas are certainly dangerous to feed, but the same can be said of any over ripe fruit, particularly pears and melons. Actually bananas are often quite firm inside even though the skins may be black, and it is only the bruised and damaged areas which become soft and rotten. Pears and melons ripen rapidly in a warm room and are dangerous to use as their high acid content undergoes a chemical change. The regular provision of tomatoes, which are rich in vitamin C, makes it unnecessary to feed oranges.

For the frugivorous species the fruit should be fortified with a mineral salt and vitamin supplement and also by the addition of protein. As many fruit pigeons and touracos will not accept insectile mixtures it is advisable to improve their diet by adding the dry insectile mixture to their fruit, in the ratio of approximately 20% insectile mixture to 80% diced fruit, which should provide sufficient protein and vitamins. Some fruit pigeons accept poultry growers' pellets mixed with their fruit. Layers' pellets should not be used as they have a higher calcium content. Boiled rice and maize have figured in fruit pigeon diets but are unnecessary if sufficient energy providing foods such as sultanas, currants and bananas are given, as they are sedentary birds which take little exercise. Dates and similar sticky foods should be avoided.

Touracos are slow to accept live food, but the colies, most fruit pigeons and the frugivorous barbets are usually interested in maggots and mealworms.

The Omnivorous Softbills

As a group the omnivorous softbills combine the feeding habits of the fruit eaters with those of the insectivorous species, sometimes even to the extent of hawking insects, as the yellow-billed hornbill and some of the bulbuls do. In the natural state their food intake varies considerably and in some species fruit forms the major part of the diet, while in others insects predominate, with an intermediate group which consume approximately equal quantities of fruit and animal food. It is not suggested of course that a bird knowingly regulates its daily intake to a particular percentage of both plant and animal matter. There may be days when insects are plentiful, and yet other days when perhaps a fruiting tree is visited regularly for several days and

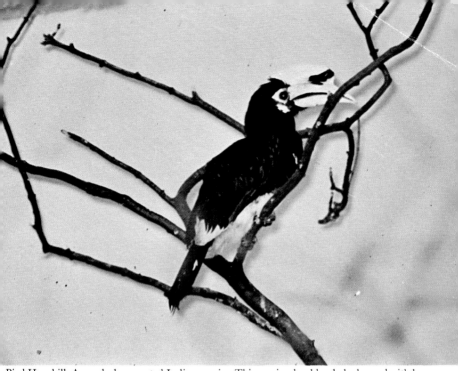

Pied Hornbill. A regularly exported Indian species. This species should only be housed with large softbills such as Jays, Jay Thrushes and Fruit Pigeons. It has a definite need for animal protein.

Below, Red-headed Manakin. Few of these humid Amazonian Forest gems reach the premises of aviculturists, due to the problems associated with their establishment. They actually thrive once established but their diet must include ample animal protein.

Spreo Starlings. The most colourful of the regularly available Glossy Starlings. A hardy bird, it can be safely wintered out when acclimatised.

Below, Lesser Green Broadbill. The only species available to aviculturists. A good insectile mixture, diced fruit and a few mealworms daily will maintain its condition. The other Broadbills are highly insectivorous, some even being insect hawkers.

Greater Rufous Motmot. The most impressive member of the group, it is easy to maintain once established. They constantly burrow when kept over deep soil.

White-browed Blue Flycatcher. An occasionally imported Asiatic species which is rather delicate and completely inoffensive. It is hardly a beginners bird, and perhaps surprisingly, does not appear to favour conservatory aviary conditions.

berries are gorged at the expense of other foods.

The omnivorous species which favour fruit are obviously adapted to survive on a diet slightly lower in calorie content, and should be given approximately 70% fruit, 25% of the insectile mixture and minced meat which is outlined in appendix B, and 5% insects. The cotingas, manakins, most tanagers and bulbuls, the toucans and some hornbills (the trumpeter and crested species for example) should be included in this group of softbills. If the insectile mixture is not readily accepted it can be mixed with the diced fruit, or rolled into small balls for the larger species, and offered as early in the day as possible before the main fruit meal is given. Toucans, cotingas and manakins are seldom interested in maggots but will accept mealworms readily enough. Some of the smaller members of this group have difficulty in digesting blowfly maggots and if possible should be given housefly maggots. Nectar, if purely honey and water, is an unnecessary addition if birds are receiving the diet outlined above, as this will provide additional fattening nutrients and little else. Also, it is often favoured by manakins and tangers to the extent of causing digestive disturbances. The larger species of cotingas, i.e. the cocks of the rock (although some authors place them in a separate family nowadays), should be offered young mice and are also fond of snails.

Most of the members of the oriolidae, icteridae and sturnidae families require a ration comprising equal parts of fruit and more nutritious foods. The birds needing such a diet form the largest group of omnivorous softbills and encompass the orioles, marshbirds, troupials, mynahs and starlings; and the birds of paradise, jays, tree pies, the American trogons and most species of arboreal hornbills. Their diet should consist of approximately 50% fruit, 40% insectile mixture and minced meat, and 10% insects. A number of the American icterids such as the military starlings, cowbirds and meadowlarks, should be offered mixed seed instead of fruit. The birds of paradise, jays and tree pies should be provided with ample roughage in the form of small mice and day old chicks.

The more insectivorous members of this group of softbills need a diet of 50% insectile mixture with minced meat, 30% live food and 20% fruit. The whiskered, grey-headed and swallow tanagers, black and yellow broadbill, violet-backed starling and salvins barbet are typical of the smaller members of this group. The red-billed, great Indian and white-crested hornbills, crows and ravens are characteristic of the larger members and these should receive in addition, perhaps every other day, small furred or feathered vertebrates. The larger hornbills and the corvids can easily cope with adult mice.

The Insectivorous Softbills

These are the softbills which are dependent upon insects in the wild state, although this diet may be supplemented with other forms of invertebrate life such as spiders, worms and snails; and even vertebrates in the form of small reptiles and amphibians. The larger the species the more likely are vertebrates to be included in the diet, but these birds cannot be classed as carnivorous species as insects form the bulk of their natural food intake.

Owing to their specialised feeding habits a number of the members of this group are difficult to establish. The todies, bee-eaters, jacamars and a few similar species are accustomed to hawking insects, and they do not readily accept cage or aviary conditions. As they show no interest in inanimate foods they are often forced to live on a diet of maggots and mealworms. Conversely, many of the insectivorous species make extremely good avicultural subjects, so much so that redstarts, niltavas, robin chats and some species of flycatchers have even bred in captivity.

The degree of difficulty in keeping insectivorous species is therefore dependent upon their acceptance of inanimate foods, which provide a more balanced diet than maggots and mealworms. It is significant that the species which have bred in captivity are among the easiest of the insectivorous birds to establish and maintain, and were obviously receiving sufficient calcium, vitamin D and protein to form their eggs. Birds which cannot be established and receive only maggots and mealworms will seldom breed and will not remain in good condition for long. If they do breed they are almost certain to become egg bound.

The deficiencies resulting from a diet of maggots and meal-worms can best be seen in young birds reared solely upon these, due to the irregular availability of other forms of insect food, and the fact that most parent birds refuse to feed their young unless live food is in plentiful supply. The deficiency symptoms have mainly been associated with the feet and legs, these being deformed and weak, from which it is obvious that the diet was deficient not only in calcium and phosphorus, but also in the vitamin D necessary for the conversion of these minerals into bone. Such deficiencies would not be obvious in an adult bird receiving the same diet, as apart from rendering it virtually incapable of reproduction, once the bones had completed their growth very little vitamin D and minerals would be needed; whereas the growing bird would need relatively large quantities of each. This can be more readily appreciated when it is known that the skeletal system contains 99% of the calcium present in vertebrates, and approximately 80% of the phosphorus. In addition, fledglings have shown muscular inco-ordination very similar to the condition occurring in poultry and known to be caused by a deficiency of vitamin E.

To substantiate the assumptions regarding the unsuitability of maggots and mealworms as a complete diet, samples have been submitted for biochemical analysis, which has proved conclusively that they contain insignificant amounts of calcium and phosphorus (see Appendix B), almost certainly insufficient to raise young birds. This lack of ash could have been foreseen anyway as insect larvae, lacking a skeletal system, might theoretically contain only similar quantities to those present in the body (muscle) of vertebrates, i.e. 1% of the calcium content and 20% of the phosphorus content. The analysis of these larvae brings to light some very interesting facts. Maggots for instance contain two thirds of the oil content of mealworms, which are 12% oil. This is not particularly high, and would hardly constitute an excess of energy foods if birds were fed solely upon mealworms, as their carbohydrate content is practically nil, and the calorie content is therefore only about 200 calories per 100 gm. of food. This is surely not too high for a purely insectivorous bird, as a diet of 80% of most energy rich insectile mixtures, together with 20% maggots and mealworms would provide more energy, and consequently more likelihood of obesity and apoplexy.

Neither can the mealworm's 20% protein content be considered excessive, as it will be seen from appendix B that the average protein content of blowflies, their maggots and house crickets is 18%, and these insects resemble the flies, caterpillars and orthopterous insects (locusts and grasshoppers) which are available to the wild bird, and which possibly have a similar content. In any case several commercial insectile mixtures have a protein content of over 20%. There is more likelihood therefore of vitamin deficiencies occurring if insectivorous species are fed solely on mealworms, than there is of obesity and gout. Naturally it is not advocated that mealworms should be the sole food of any captive bird or the staff of life. The above facts and assumptions have been given as an indication that mealworms are not as rich as is commonly believed.

If insectivorous species are receiving a complete diet, a few mealworms daily will provide a welcome change from maggots and insectile mixture, and may also act as a breeding stimulant. For the species that will not accept inanimate foods a diet of maggots and mealworms, while deficient in other respects, will not be too "rich". This is not so with the frugivorous and omnivorous species however, as their fat and protein requirements appear to be lower, and the addition of too many mealworms to the daily food ration can be both over-stimulating and fattening.

Assessing the vitamin content of live foods is unfortunately a complex and costly undertaking, and until more work is done in this field, assumption, which has so often played a large part in aviculture, must still be offered until analyses have proved the point. It seems reasonable to assume that maggots and mealworms are deficient in vitamins A and D, and no doubt in others too. The vitamin D deficiency symptoms have already been discussed in relation to the rearing of young birds, and many adult birds fed solely on these larvae have shown evidence of avitaminosis A. The symptoms of this deficiency are watering eyes, asthmatic breathing and eventual death from enteritis, and in the past have been attributed to something present in the larvae fed to the birds, as opposed to something missing. Wattle-eyed and other flycatchers showing these symptoms have responded to massive oral doses of vitamin A, given direct into the beak as they seem disinclined to drink. Possibly in the wild state the semi-digested carotene rich plant material in the gut of caterpillars and locusts provides the bird with sufficient vitamin A, as carotene can be converted into this. Vitamin D can be manufactured by a bird upon exposure to sunlight of the naked areas of its body, but how an insectivorous bird obtains other vitamins, and indeed the calcium and phosphorus necessary for rearing its young, in the wild state is certainly puzzling.

Although it is possible to obtain insectile mixtures commercially, it is far more satisfactory to prepare one's own, as the composition can then be altered to cope with varying climatic conditions and different methods of housing. The ingredients used can vary slightly in composition depending upon where they were grown and when they were harvested, in the case of cereals; and the type of product used in the case of meals of animal origin, but these variations are insignificant and will not greatly alter the final analysis of the mixture.

The protein content of a replacement mixture can be provided by dried flies, fish meal, meat and bone meal, shrimp meal, dried yeast or ant pupae, all of which are available commercially. It is better to use several of these products than a single one. A good quality fish or meat meal of British origin should be chosen, and meat and bone meal should be used in moderation due to its high calcium content. Dried flies and ant pupae (eggs) are not as useless nutritionally as is often thought, as blowflies which have had their moisture content removed artificially have been found to contain 50% protein. It is reasonable therefore, to assume that the Chinese dried flies must contain a similar amount if they have been dried artificially or slightly less if they have been air dried, as less moisture would then have been removed. They undoubtedly provide a lot of protein, but their high cost makes them uneconomical and they can be satisfactorily replaced with a good quality meat meal. As the crushed bodies of the small Chinese flies bear little resemblance to an insect, particularly when included in an insectile mixture, the argument that some birds will only accept such mixtures when flies are included is hardly valid.

Ants' eggs, in reality the cocoon and enclosed pupae of the ant, must contain less protein and digestible components as almost half their weight is made up of woven cocoon, which is still of animal origin of course, although it is doubtful if it is fully digestible. They too are an expensive source of protein.

Biscuit meal is frequently used to provide the bulk and carbohydrate portion of the mixture, plus any of the cereal meals—barley, maize, wholemeal, soya flour etc.—which have a high energy content. Sweet biscuit meal should be avoided as it will probably contain unspecified amounts of fat or oil and sugar used in biscuit making.

There is a great deal in favour of providing insectivorous birds with a diet low in energy foods and rich in protein, whereas most diets may contain sufficient protein but are certainly excessive from the energy-providing point of view. The calorific content of fats and oils is double that of the sugars, starches and protein, and if corn oils or dripping are used for moistening insectile mixtures the energy content of the ration will be fantastically high, as these fats and oils contain 99% pure oil. Honey contains only 76% carbohydrate, and therefore provides less than half the amount of energy. There is evidence of course that birds cannot deal with large amounts of fats or oils.

Although honey is the best mixing agent due to its lower calorie content, palatability and the ease with which it is assimilated, it is likely to dry out in high temperatures. On the other hand if oils are used the mixtures should be freshly made at least every other day, as the unsaturated fatty acids cause oxidation of vitamins A and E. If it is intended to store an oil mixed food for any time an anti-oxidant should be added.

The ingredients already mentioned do not contain sufficient vitamins or mineral salts, except calcium and phosphorus in the case of the meat and bone and fish meals, and a supplement should therefore be added to the insectile mixture.

In addition to the insectile mixture raw meat plays an important part in practically all insectivorous bird diets. Raw minced beef is most often used, but being poor in all vitamins and mineral salts it should always be fortified with a vitamin and mineral salt supplement. To simplify the preparation of food it is a good idea to mix the minced meat with the insectile mixture daily, and this can be done after the addition of the honey, if several days supply of the basic mixture is made at one time. Or it can completely replace the honey, and will provide a friable mixture with a lower carbohydrate content. This method of feeding will also supply a more complete diet for all the insectivorous species housed in community aviaries, as it is well known that some may concentrate upon minced meat for instance, at the expense of the mixture, if they are fed separately. Although it may seem wasteful to feed birds in this manner, (because of the necessity of discarding any food left at the end of the day, whereas insectile mixtures are normally left for several days until eaten) it does not take long to judge the birds' intake fairly accurately, and the supply can be regulated accordingly. The fact that the birds are known to be eating a suitable diet, and the avoidance of having deteriorating mixtures left before them for several days, more than offsets any small wastage incurred.

For most species a mixture of two parts insectile mixture and one part raw minced meat by volume has been found satisfactory, but the percentage of meat should be increased for the larger species such as rollers and motmots. As the protein and fat content of both raw meat and the insectile mixture outlined in appendix B are similar, any variations of the percentages of each used will not significantly alter the composition of the diet.

The Carnivorous Softbills

The softbills which feed mainly upon vertebrates are considered
to be carnivorous, and although at first glance it may appear
that the species included in this group are hardly softbilled
birds, they satisfy the requirements of the definition given in
chapter 1, and are all members of families of accepted softbills,
differing only in having a more specialised diet. They are mainly
zoological garden exhibits.

Most of the carnivorous species are fish-eating kingfishers
which range in size from the small malachite kingfishers to the
giant kingfisher. Many of these also catch other water creatures
such as shrimps, crabs, tadpoles and occasionally insects. Other
birds within this group live mainly upon small terrestrial
vertebrates such as rodents, lizards, small snakes and young
birds, and they are the greater roadrunner, several species of
shrikes, the ground hornbills and the kookaburra, all of which
are decidedly carnivorous.

In captivity the fish eaters should receive strips of meat
and suitably sized fish. Small whitebait are suitable for the
malachite and common kingfishers, and sprats for the larger
storkbilled and giant kingfishers. The smaller species can
sometimes be induced to accept insects as well, although it is
more often necessary to use live fish to stimulate these birds into
feeding at all. Whole fish should form the larger part of the diet
as they are a more complete food than strips of fish or meat. The
addition of a vitamin and mineral salt supplement is a problem
as it is normal procedure to place both fish and strips of meat in
water to avoid drying out and to stimulate feeding. It is possible,
however, to insert this supplement into small mice for the larger
kingfishers, and to inject minute quantities of the liquid form
into mealworms for the small kingfishers. Some species may
accept shrimps and small crabs.

The insectile mixture described in appendix B with additional
minced meat should be accepted by the roadrunners, shrikes,
kookaburras and hornbills. If not, pieces of raw meat for the

agpie Jay. A distinctive member of the bird fauna of the more arid regions of Mexico the agpie Jay makes an attractive addition to any bird collection. Typical of the Crow family it s aggressive tendencies and should not be housed with smaller birds.

Fairy Bluebird. Undoubtedly the most attractive of the readily available, low priced softbi
It is easy to maintain, is not aggressive to smaller birds and has bred on numerous occasions
captivity.

latter and small strips for the others are suitable, in each case following the standard procedure of adding vitamins and mineral salts. In addition suitably sized mice and dismembered day old chicks can be offered the shrikes, while all the others are quite capable of dealing with these whole.

ADDITIONAL BIRD FOODS

In addition to the bird foods and mixtures already mentioned in the preceding pages, many others are, or have been, used for feeding softbilled birds. Some of these are as follows:

Eggs
It is common policy to add hard-boiled egg to a prepared insectile mixture. While being a highly nutritious food, and of great value in tempting birds to accept inanimate foods, it should be remembered that egg is in its most indigestible form when hard boiled, and is most digestible when coddled. The practice of moistening foods with beaten raw egg is unwise also, as the toxic substance avidin which is present in raw egg white renders the biotin of the egg yolk useless, causing biotin deficiency. Avidin is destroyed when eggs are lightly cooked. In addition moistened egg foods sour very quickly in warm temperatures, and pathogenic organisms are soon in appearance. It is therefore risky to use egg in insectile mixtures in conservatory aviaries where there is the possibility of uneaten food particles being left in the soil.

Other Meat
Raw beef heart is often used because of its low fat content, but it is not a particularly good bird food as it contains the anti-vitamin thiaminase, which deactivates the thiamine in the diet. Deficiency of this vitamin can cause digestive disturbances and poor metabolism of energy foods, and stunted growth.

Horse meat has a coarser grain than beef and contains less fat, but has a higher acid content. Whale meat has been used in the past although it is doubtful whether the need, through shortage of domestic meat or the over-abundance of whales, will ever arise again. The feeding of whale meat over a fairly long period was thought to have caused paralysis and eventual death of a number of birds at the Philadelphia Zoo some years ago.

Fish
Strangely the flesh of the white fish—cod, halibut, hake etc.—is very low in vitamin content, in fact devoid of some, and yet their livers are the richest natural source of vitamins A and D. The flesh of the fatty fish (herrings, sprats and whitebait) is fairly rich in both these vitamins. The protein content of raw fish is high and is comparable to that of raw meat, but the higher fat content of the fatty fish compares with that of cheese.

Cheese
Cheese is a very good food for most softbills, but as it is rich in fat as well as having a high protein content it should be used in moderation. Dried cheese, which has had most of the oil extracted would be a highly suitable food. A typical soft cheese contains about 28% protein and 30% fat, and is very rich in vitamin A.

Rice
Rice is a good energy providing food but in the polished form is devoid of vitamins A, D, C and B_{12} and the others are poorly represented. The protein content is very low, and as energy providing foods seem to be the last thing that most birds require in addition to the diets already outlined, there is little point in feeding rice.

Dog Biscuits
Many aviculturists feed their omnivorous birds, particularly starlings, on soaked dog biscuits of the more nutritious grades instead of raw meat. The reason is in order not to provide an excess of protein, as too much is considered unsuitable for such birds and leads to gout. It is true that they do not need excessive

quantities of protein or raw meat, and the diet outlined for them contains less than 15% meat, but the addition of dog biscuits is likely to increase the protein content, as many contain over 20% protein.

Colour Foods

It is a well known fact that birds with red, pink or yellow feathering cannot produce these pigments unaided, and fade in captivity unless provided with a colour holding agent. The cocks of the rock, Baltimore orioles, minivets and scarlet-chested sunbirds are typical examples. Many colour foods have been used, but concentrated carrot oil, ground red pepper and the synthetic canthaxanthin have produced good results.

Live Foods

While the inclusion of certain food nutrients in softbills' diets is perhaps questionable, the fact that live food is essential to maintain the health of all the insectivorous species, and most of the omnivorous, carnivorous and nectivorous birds too, is indisputable.

Apart from the drosophila mentioned in connection with the food intake of nectivorous birds, the insects referred to so far have been maggots and mealworms, as these are the only forms of live food readily available to aviculture. In addition to these larvae however, other forms of live food are occasionally available, some seasonally, a few commercially. Of the latter it is possible to purchase the small white worm enchytrae and the earthworm from live-bait supply firms. The minute enchytrae are only suitable for the smallest and more delicate insectivorous species, whereas earthworms are readily accepted by many birds, particularly thrushes and pittas. Unless large quantities of earthworms are needed, sufficient can usually be obtained during the summer months by laying a damp sack on a lawn, or the greens of a golf course. Many worms will gather beneath this overnight.

Frogs can be purchased from laboratory supply firms for the larger carnivorous birds, but they are likely to be rather expensive. Both bee and wasp larvae are known to be highly nutritious foods, yet the author's experience is that few birds are interested in the plump, thin-skinned larvae. Perhaps it is an acquired taste. Aviculturists living in or near the countryside can often supplement their birds' diets with locally available live foods, as a short walk through woodland can provide a good crop of snails, woodlice, ant pupae and beetle larvae etc, if every piece of rotting wood or slab of rock is turned over.

Other forms of live food can be produced with little trouble and small outlay, and the species that have a relatively short life cycle are obviously the most suitable. These include housefly larvae, blowflies, crickets, cockroaches, locusts, waxmoths etc. The undesirability of both crickets and cockroaches as house pests is a deterrent however, unless isolated quarters can be provided. The most economical methods of producing these insects are as follows:

Blowflies

Blowflies are a good source of protein for birds, and provide also the interest and stimulation which are missing from a dish of maggots. They are seldom used however due to the difficulty of feeding them alive, and much of their benefit is lost if they are killed before being used. They can be immobilised by refrigeration, but there is possibly some risk involved if large numbers of ice-cold flies are eaten.

Hawking species can be catered for by allowing the flies to escape from their container through a small hole in the lid, which allows only one out at a time. Other softbills soon develop the habit of sitting on the container's edge waiting for the flies to appear.

A high protein food mixture is essential for producing and rearing blowfly maggots, and the smell of decomposing meat or fermenting artificial mixtures, such as milk powder, yeast and meat meal, is sufficient deterrent. They can be reared on autoclaved meat to eliminate smell, but this would be rather expensive. The efforts to produce blowfly maggots are hardly worthwhile anyway as they are always available commercially. However they are obtained it is essential that they are allowed to "clean" themselves in bran or sawdust in a warm room, before they are given to the birds. Two days should be allowed for them to remove all traces of food in the gut.

When flies are needed the maggots should be allowed to pupate in shallow trays, and then must be separated from the bran or sawdust, which can be blown off. The pupae should then be placed in layers alternating with layers of coarse sand in clean tins or jars, with ample air holes in the lids. The sand should be moistened daily. At 75°F blowfly pupae take approximately seven days to hatch, but it is essential that they are kept moist. If they are exposed to warm air they quickly dehydrate and will not hatch. On no account must they be allowed to pupate in the bran or sawdust in which they have cleaned themselves, as by the time the flies are ready to emerge the contents of the hatching tin will have become a damp, evil-smelling· mass, and worse still a source of infection. Cases of bacterial infection and consequent heavy losses amongst insectivorous species have resulted from feeding flies which had been contaminated by pupating in this manner.

Houseflies

The smaller softbilled birds often have difficulty in digesting the tough-skinned blowfly maggots, and housefly larvae have proved entirely suitable for them. Housefly eggs hatch in 24 hours, and the fast growing larvae are ready to pupate after eight days. At 75°F it takes six days for the pupae to hatch, and the flies are ready to lay their eggs four days later. Like most insects their life cycle is accelerated when the temperature is increased, and is extended by lower temperatures.

The breeding houseflies can be kept in any container provided it is flyproofed with gauze or muslin. Plywood boxes have been equipped with a "sleeve" to facilitate feeding and egg removal, and have proved entirely suitable. Small dishes of cotton wool soaked with milk can be provided as a source of food for the flies, and they will also lay their eggs on this. Before they become dehydrated the eggs must be removed and placed in the rearing medium comprising equal parts by volume of wheat bran and poultry pellets, moistened with water. The moisture content of the medium is in fact the most critical factor in the production of housefly larvae. It should be moist and crumbly when first mixed, and should be allowed to dry out on top as the larvae mature. A deep bowl or tin containing about

6 in. depth of the medium will allow the top to dry without affecting the moisture content of the lower layers. As the larvae mature they migrate to the top, dry layer to pupate.

Fruitflies

Due to the ease with which they can be bred and their very short life cycle, fruitflies or drosophila are bred domestically more than any other insect reared for bird feeding. Many relatively complicated mixtures of yeast, sugar and agar have been used for breeding these flies in the laboratory, but as every softbill enthusiast is aware, they breed freely upon waste fruit. At 75°F their complete life cycle is only about seven days, and this appears to be the most suitable temperature for breeding them. Above 80°F there is a very definite reduction in the breeding rate.

Vestigial winged mutant fruitflies are particularly useful for feeding to the small delicate birds which are unable to catch the winged flies.

Locusts

Locusts in their varying sizes are an ideal food for a wide range of birds. The newly hatched hoppers are a convenient size for the smallest and most delicate insectivorous species, and the coarse bodied adults are excellent for motmots, rollers and similar large softbills. They are relatively easy to breed if the correct temperature is maintained, and at 85°F their life cycle is approximately 10 weeks. At this temperature eggs take about 14 days to hatch, and the non-flying juvenile stages undergo five moults, the first four at intervals of 5 days, and the last after 7 days. Mature females commence laying about 4 weeks after their last moult.

Several laboratory supply firms include locust breeding cages in their range of equipment, but simple plywood boxes, equipped with a perforated zinc front, and a sleeved opening for servicing have proved entirely satisfactory. Fresh young grass, placed in small pots of water, is the most suitable food for locusts, but they also eat bran, apple and carrot. During the winter months it is a good idea to sprout corn or bird seed to supplement the poor quality grass.

Locusts must be provided with suitable containers for egg deposition, and small plastic lunch boxes filled with coarse sand have been used with great success. The egg masses can be seen through the plastic at the bottom of the box and sometimes at the sides also. When sufficient have been laid the container should be removed to cages designated for hatching and rearing. Once again, the moisture content of the sand is the most critical factor. It should be moist, but not saturated, as this will rot the eggs. The top $\frac{1}{2}$ in. of sand should be allowed to dry before the contents are moistened again.

Mealworms

The food requirements of the mealworm are relatively simple, and they are easy to breed with very little effort providing the correct heat and degree of humidity is maintained. They will not thrive if they are kept very hot and dry, as the eggs will be dehydrated before they can hatch. This may occur if bran is used as a rearing medium, as little moisture is retained by the loose flakes. Barley meal has been used with good results as it provides the fine meal needed by the minute newly hatched larvae. A depth of several inches of this meal will ensure that the moisture content remains fairly high. Additional moisture can be provided in the form of slices of apple or carrot, or banana skins, which also serve as food for the final stage in this insects life cycle—the stored grain beetle. An excess of these high moisture foods however must not come into contact with the meal as they will encourage the growth of mould. They are best placed on top of several layers of hessian, which can also be lightly sprayed with water every other day. At 80°F the life cycle of the stored grain beetle is about 4 months, but this can be delayed at any stage by reducing the temperature.

Other forms of live food can be reared for tropical birds but their small size and more exacting food requirements do not make them very attractive propositions. The wax moth needs a mixture of oats, honey and glycerine, and both the larvae and moth are rather small. The confused flour beetle requires similar treatment to the mealworm, but the adult larvae are very small. Either of these insects could be replaced with housefly larvae and small mealworms, both of these being less trouble to produce.

Ailments and their Treatment

The need for a bird to maintain its body temperature has already been stressed, and at no time is this more essential than when its condition is lowered by disease. When it is obvious that a bird is ill and requires treatment the first action to take is to provide for it a temperature of 85°F (29·4°C). Hospital cages complete with thermostat are available commercially, but can be quite easily constructed from a wooden box with a sliding glass front and sufficient ventilation holes, and equipped with an overhead electric light bulb of suitable wattage to give the required temperature at perch level. A wire partition should separate birds from the light bulb. The hospital cage should always be placed in a separate room or quarantine quarters away from other birds in case the ailment should be infectious.

As sick birds are more likely to drink than eat, their water supply is the ideal medium for the introduction of drugs. Distilled or boiled water should always be used for this purpose, and only in glass, china or enamel containers, as the use of metal dishes may cause a chemical reaction when certain drugs are used. Nectar or other easily assimilated foods should be provided, and if possible a vitamin supplement introduced when the drug treatment has ceased.

It is often a difficult task to diagnose bird ailments as the symptoms of many diseases are very similar. Where diagnosis is uncertain a veterinary surgeon should be consulted, rather than start a course of treatment based upon guesswork, which could do more harm than good. With some infections a correct diagnosis is impossible and the nature of the infection can only be determined by post mortem examination.

For ease of reference the following bird ailments have been grouped according to their main external symptoms or to the area of the bird affected by the ailment.

Ailments affecting the alimentary system

(a) *Looseness of the bowel*

It must be remembered that softbills normally have soft and sometimes semi-liquid droppings due to the nature of their diet. Looseness of the bowel, when the droppings are almost watery, can be due to non-infectious causes such as malnutrition, contaminated food or to using dirty utensils. In these instances the diarrhoea is not a disease symptom as it is not caused by pathogenic organisms. It is wise to administer a few drops of a mild aperient—olive oil, medicinal paraffin etc., to clear the digestive tract before giving an oral astringent to check the looseness. A little powdered chalk, bismuth or tincture of catechu is usually effective.

If the condition is not improved by this treatment it must be considered to be infectious in origin, and it is advisable to seek professional advice as it could be caused by a number of organisms. Unfortunately these cannot be accurately identified until after death, when microscopical examination can be carried out. If death occurs after a severe bout of diarrhoea the following organisms should be suspected and a post mortem examination arranged without delay.

Salmonella pullorum is the bacteria responsible for the disease known as bacillary white diarrhoea, in which the symptoms are a thoroughly dejected appearance and a yellowish white diarrhoea which sticks to the feathers and often blocks the cloaca. It is highly infectious, but has been effectively treated with the drug furazolidone.

Salmonella typhimurum causes paratyphoid or salmonellosis. The symptoms of white coloured diarrhoea and dejection do not last long as death usually occurs within a few days. It is extremely infectious and is often carried by rats and mice. Eggs which have been infected by the droppings of contaminated hens also help to spread the disease.

Several members of the genus *eimeria* cause coccidiosis, which is fatal unless the correct treatment is administered very quickly. Infections frequently occur when birds are housed upon ground which has previously been contaminated by poultry. The symptoms are similar to those of bacillary white diarrhoea, the droppings being white and often bloodstained. Infected birds have a dejected, drooping appearance. Sulphonamides and nitrofurazone have been successful in treating this infection.

Escherichia coli is an organism which is normally present in birds' intestines, but flares into disease producing proportions at times of stress and when a bird's resistance is low, particularly during shipment and at times of overcrowding. The antibiotics aureomycin and terramycin have produced good results in treating this infection.

(b) *Constipation*

Constipation is caused by the excessive drying out of food material in the gut, forming an impacted mass. It is normally due to faulty nutrition, when there is insufficient bulk or roughage in the diet, but is seldom a problem with softbilled birds. A lubricant should be given, preferably cod liver oil, olive oil or liquid paraffin, and the vent should be massaged with olive oil, gently forcing out the obstruction. On no account should pressure, however gentle, be used on the abdomen, in the hope that this will force out the obstruction.

(c) *Eggbinding*

This condition seldom causes concern in softbill collections. It can arise from sudden changes of temperature when a bird is about to lay, from having insufficient calcium in the diet, from lack of exercise or through attempting to lay an oversized egg. The affected bird will strain occasionally although in a very weak condition, and a bulge will be seen just inside the cloaca. This will indicate the position of the egg, probably firmly held by the sphincter muscle separating the oviduct from the cloaca. Olive oil should be gently introduced into the cloaca and around the egg with a soft feather, whilst the bird is held over a bowl of steaming water, and the egg gently forced out, taking care not to break it. The bird should be allowed to recover in a temperature of not less than 80°F (26·5°C).

Convulsions and Fits

The most common cause of fits and convulsions which are often fatal is the condition known as apoplexy. This is brought about by obesity caused through lack of exercise and a diet too rich in energy foods. The haemorrhage which occurs sometimes results in paralysis of the legs or wings due to a blood clot. Birds occasionally recover if treated quickly with Epsom salts, which assists the rapid loss of weight necessary. A diet low in carbohydrates and fats should be fed and the bird disturbed as little as possible. This condition is hardly likely to occur amongst birds housed outdoors during the winter.

Epileptic fits are unlikely to be troublesome to softbill keepers as they occur mainly in weak handreared birds that have not received a correct diet.

A deficiency of vitamin D may produce convulsions, in addition to loss of appetite and digestive upsets. A complete absence of this vitamin in a bird's diet would soon result in death.

Nostrils and Breathing

Aspergillosis, the scourge of captive penguins, sometimes occurs in softbill collections. It is caused by the fungus *aspergillus fumigatus* which infects the lungs. The symptoms are gasping and wheezing and there is occasionally a discharge from the nostrils. A post mortem examination is necessary before a definite diagnosis can be made, and when this has been confirmed all possible precautionary sterilisation measures should be carried out to prevent further losses.

Catarrh is also symptomised by a discharge from the nostrils and eyes and wheezing, but this can be due to exposure to draughts or bad weather. Friars balsam in hot water is a good inhalant and assists in reducing the inflammation of the mucous membranes. The eyes and nostrils should be bathed with a boracic solution. If untreated this condition can cause serious impaction of the sinuses, which in small birds are almost impossible to clear.

The common cold, caused by a sudden drop in temperature, exposure to draughts or bathing in cold water just before roosting, can develop into pneumonia if untreated. When this happens the hoarseness develops into the rapid breathing and sneezing associated with pneumonia. A course of terramycin or aureomycin should be given immediately the condition is noticed, and the patient removed to a hospital cage and high temperatures without delay. It should remain there until the symptoms have subsided.

Asthmatic wheezing is normally a symptom of the infections already described, as opposed to being a specific ailment.

The presence of a small lung parasite known to science as *Syngamus trachealis* causes a condition commonly known as gapes, which is characterized by gaping and coughing, and in advanced cases, by harsh wheezing. The eggs of this worm are coughed up from the windpipe, swallowed and passed out with the droppings, contaminating the floor of their quarters and exposing other birds to the infection. Thiabenzole has produced remarkable results in eradicating this parasite.

Skin and Feathers

Plucking by other birds seldom occurs in collections of softbilled birds, and when it does the only remedy is to remove the culprit and house it on its own. Self-feather plucking is also an uncommon habit and can be caused by an infection of the depluming mite *Cnemidocoptes levis*, which cannot be seen as they infect the feather quills within the epidermis. They cause such intense irritation that the bird pulls out or breaks off the affected feathers. The affected area of skin should be washed with soapy water containing sulphur.

Newly imported birds may arrive infected with feather lice, which can easily be seen attached to the feathers when the birds are closely examined. They are not blood-suckers but live on the feathers and dead skin, although they have been known to bite into living cells and consume blood. Their presence in quantity causes skin irritations and dry, brittle feathers due to the oil having been eaten. They can easily be eradicated with one of the many bird sprays available commercially.

A bird's inability to complete its moult is frequently caused by a drastic change of temperature during moulting, but it can also be due to malnutrition, particularly lack of protein. As moulting places a great strain upon birds they should receive a very liberal diet and should not be subjected to any stresses. Holding the caged bird over a steaming dish of water for a few minutes, or increasing the temperature to hospital cage proportions are the best methods of ensuring a continuation of the moult.

Skin tumours can appear almost anywhere, whereas feather cysts are usually confined to the more densely feathered areas. The bacterial infections of the leg joints, which often result in tumours, have responded to a course of treatment with terramycin. Both skin tumours and feather cysts should be painted with an astringent such as tincture of iodine or friars balsam, and if they are open should be gently squeezed out.

Feet and Legs

Gout is symptomised by swollen toes and lameness, and in the more commonly seen form can be confirmed by the swollen abdomen caused by malfunction of the kidneys. An excess of protein, deficiency of vitamins and lack of exercise can cause this ailment. A very light diet should be given to affected birds, and a small quantity of sodium bicarbonate added to their drinking water. The affected toes should be painted with iodine.

Dietary disturbances can also result in the condition known as bumblefoot, which is characterised by swollen feet and abscesses under the toes. In this instance an excessive oil intake can be the cause, although it is sometimes induced by incorrect perching. The treatment involves lancing the abscess and expelling the contents, after which it should be painted with an astringent.

A small mite, which cannot be seen with the naked eye, burrows under the leg scales and causes the condition known as scaly leg. The infected leg scales become thicker and harder than normal, but a few applications of olive oil are usually sufficient to destroy the mite, by which time the softened scales can be easily removed.

Anaemia

Anaemia is symptomised by dejection, dullness and listlessness and can be caused by the following infections.

(a) *Avian tuberculosis*

Infected birds are emaciated and listless, and as the disease progresses they become very inactive. Unfortunately a definite diagnosis can only be made after a post mortem examination has been carried out. There is no successful treatment and complete sterilisation of utensils and quarters should be carried out when an outbreak has been confirmed. The infection can remain active in soil and buildings for a considerable time.

(b) *Red Mite*

Red mite infection is probably the most common cause of anaemia and dejection among softbills, particularly those newly arrived from South America. They are modified for blood sucking, and a heavy infestation can rapidly seriously lower a bird's vitality. The commercially available sprays for both birds and cages are the most effective method of eradication.

(c) *Internal parasites*

Both roundworms and tapeworms infect cage birds, and where the former are present mature whole worms can be found in the droppings. Roundworms are mainly free-living in the gut, but the scolex or head of the tapeworm is buried in the intestinal epithelium, and only the mature egg-filled segments at the tail end of the worm are passed out with the droppings. Consequently the tapeworms are more difficult to remove than

Violet Euphonia. A commonly available small Tanager from northern South America, it will thrive on the standard omnivorous softbill fare of finely diced fruit, insectile mixture and a little live food.

White-headed Touraco. Although the common Green Crested Touracos have proved extremely destructive in conservatory aviaries, this species and the Red-Crested Touracos are less harmful to plants. Basically a frugivorous bird in the wild state. it's diet in captivity must include animal protein.

roundworms, as the head is often left attached to the gut lining after a course of treatment and soon grows more segments. As tapeworms require an intermediate host before they can infect other birds there is little chance of captive birds becoming infected. Thiabenzole, used successfully in treating tapeworm infestations is equally successful in removing intestinal parasites, as also are the piperazine compounds.

After mite and worm infestations it is wise to administer a tonic in the form of a few drops of citrate of iron or sulphate of iron.

Mouth

Thrush is the common name for an infection of the mouth by the fungus *candida albicans*. The symptoms are a greyish white membranous coating, the area underneath being ulcerated. For mild cases a few crystals of potassium permanganate dissolved in water have produced a cure. For more serious infections the drug mycostatin should be used, as this has been developed for treating this and other fungal infections.

In softbilled birds the avian diphtheria infection occurs mainly in the form of lesions in the mouth. These are filled with a substance resembling cheese both in colour and texture. In the more advanced stages of this disease the bone may become infected. Often, infected birds appear to be quite normal externally until death occurs. Also known as pox or canker, this disease will respond to treatment with only the most advanced antibiotics and a veterinary surgeon should therefore be consulted.

Eyes

Conjunctivitis is an infectious ailment in which the eyes firstly water, then become swollen and closed, and are often matted with feathers. Blindness can result unless the eyes are bathed with a boracic solution, and treated with 2% yellow oxide of mercury ointment.

Running eyes are more often caused by exposure to draughts, but can be a symptom of catarrh. Bathing with boracic solution, followed by applications of golden eye ointment is usually sufficient to cure this condition.

There is no successful treatment for cataracts of the eye, where the pupils become white and opaque, and loss of sight is inevitable.

Deficiency diseases

These are due mainly to deficiences of vitamins and mineral salts, as in instances where the other food nutrients are deficient, the lowered condition of the birds would increase their susceptibility to other infections, and they would not necessarily show specific deficiency symptoms.

Unlike the ailments already listed it is considered more practical to include all deficiency diseases under one heading, rather than separate them according to the predominant symptoms. When an almost complete deficiency occurs the symptoms are well defined, and if the contents of appendix 'A' are read in conjunction with table 1, it should be possible to ascertain whether these are due to deficiencies, or can be attributed to other causes.

While complete deficiencies are often quite easily recognised, partial deficiencies may persist unrecognised and have eventual harmful effects due to the gradual loss of condition throughout a bird's life. The symptoms of vitamin and mineral deficiencies therefore vary in intensity according to the degree of deficiency.

The full vitamin and mineral salt requirements of softbilled birds are still unknown, although it can be safely assumed that all are necessary, with perhaps the exception of vitamin C. There is no reason for believing, with a few exceptions, that the ratio which has proved suitable for poultry is unsuitable for cage birds. These exceptions are, of course, the vitamin D, calcium and phosphorus content of growers and layers rations, which are not required in such quantity by adult softbills, even if they are breeding.

For ease of reference the main vitamins and their avitaminoses are given in table 1.

TABLE I

Vitamin A. Deficiency causes lowered resistance to diseases of the respiratory tract, xerophthalmia (an eye disease), enteritis and septicaemia. This vitamin is oxydised when exposed to the air, and foods containing ingredients rich in vitamin A, e.g. cod liver oil, should be mixed fresh daily.

Thiamine B_1. Deficiency of this vitamin results in stunted growth, digestive disturbances and poor metabolism of carbohydrates and fats.

Riboflavin B_2. Riboflavin is oxydised by sunlight and deficiency slows the growth rate of young birds and also causes digestive upsets. Sores at the corners of the mouth can be due to a lack of this vitamin and it is essential for correct nerve functioning.

Nicotinamide. This vitamin promotes growth and health and is essential for the correct functioning of the gastro-intestinal tract.

Pantothenic acid. The deficiency symptoms are similar to those of the other B complex vitamins above, plus poor feather development and dermatitis around the eyes.

Vitamin D. The vitamin closely associated with calcium and phosphorus metabolism, each of which must be present in the correct ratio. A deficiency of either will cause rickets, poor bone and beak growth, reduced breeding and poor hatchability. Vitamin D can be manufactured by the skin on exposure to sunlight.

Vitamin E. Deficiency causes muscular inco-ordination and skeletal anomalies in young birds similar to those caused by lack of vitamin D. The inco-ordination of movement is known as encephalomalacia or crazy chick disease, in which the head is alternately arched backwards and bent downwards.

Vitamin K. Often known as the "clotting" vitamin. A deficiency results in a tendency to haemorrhage and slowness to clot.

Insufficient calcium and phosphorus in the diet results in the same deficiency diseases as those caused by the lack of vitamin D, whereas potassium deficiency causes retarded growth in young stock, loss of the use of their legs and eventual death. Insufficient magnesium also retards growth, and death follows violent convulsions. Manganese deficiency causes perosis, a deformity of the leg bones, in which the hock joint becomes enlarged and the leg rotates outwards; whilst zinc deficiency results in poor feathering.

The administration of vitamin and mineral salt supplements to stock which will accept inanimate diets is no problem, as they can be added to their insectile or meat mixtures or sprinkled upon their diced fruit. It is often a problem however where young birds or adults will accept only live food. Here, the supplement cannot be added to the drinking water, as this will be taken neither by the nestlings, nor by such inveterate insect eaters as the bee-eaters and some flycatchers, which obtain sufficient moisture from their diet and are not known to drink.

Often only maggots and mealworms are available for these birds, whereas the provision of other insects (crickets, cockroaches, blowflies and locusts) would give a more complete diet. The symptoms frequently shown by captive bred youngsters indicate that the bone-forming minerals and vitamins are absent in addition to other vitamins, but this will not be enlarged upon here as this subject is discussed in more detail in chapter 6.

The most common methods of introducing a more nutritious element into a bird's diet usually involve high protein foods which are either fed to mealworms or powdered upon them prior to feeding. The amount of this additive in the gut of the mealworm or sticking to it externally will be minute, and the low percentage of vitamins and minerals present in this protein food is consequently reduced to infinitesimal quantities. These methods would produce better results if a highly concentrated vitamin and mineral salt supplement were used instead of a proprietary high protein baby or invalid food. However, there is no evidence that mealworms can retain or store minerals or vitamins in the tissues, and the small amount in the gut or sticking to them is probably insufficient for young birds.

With blowfly maggots it is impractical to add supplements to their diet, as the high temperatures and high protein foods they require cause the food medium either to ferment or decompose in a very short time, thereby requiring the maggots to be cleaned before being fed. Maggots, however, can be lightly coated with honey before being sprinkled with a supplement, but mealworms will die if subjected to this treatment as they are not modified for a semi-liquid existence.

Small quantities of liquid vitamins and liquid calcium can be injected into mealworms if a fine hypodermic needle is used, although the larger bodied locusts and crickets are more suitable for this.

PART II
The Groups of Softbilled Birds

The Nectivorous Softbills

The Hummingbirds

Often referred to as "living jewels" the hummingbirds really do justice to the names which have been bestowed upon them over the years, names derived from the jewels—ruby, emerald, topaz etc., and from the heavens—sunbeams, comets, angels etc. They vary in size from the bee hummingbird of Cuba and the Isle of Pines which is only $2\frac{1}{2}$ in. long, to the 8-in. long giant hummingbird found in the northern Andes of South America.

They are capable of very swift flight, can hover and fly backwards, and are without doubt one of the most highly specialised softbilled birds. Their incessant activity is powered by the intake of several times their own weight of high energy foods daily. As this results in their need to feed more frequently than any other bird, the question of how migrating ruby-throated hummingbirds can cross the Gulf of Mexico without feeding is rather puzzling. They must be able to convert, shortly before migrating, a large amount of carbohydrate into stored fat to provide the energy for the long flight, and yet in captivity a definite regulatory mechanism controls the consumption of food. The stronger the nutrient content of mixtures the lower is the intake. Obviously this regulatory mechanism must be over-ruled prior to migration. The nectar obtained by the wild bird is after all almost pure invert sugar as opposed to the well diluted substitute offered captive birds, and the intake is therefore not governed by the amount of fluids that the bird is able to cope with.

Hummingbirds are the only known birds to undergo a daily cycle of torpidity, when the body temperature is lowered and the bird becomes inactive, thereby making a considerable saving of energy. This occurs whilst they are roosting irrespective of the air temperature.

They are solitary aggressive birds and in captivity are well known for their intolerance of their own kind, intimidating their companions and driving them from the feeding tubes. Only occasionally is it possible to keep two or more together in cages or small flights.

The hummingbird family is confined to the New World, ranging from Alaska to Tierra del Fuego, but they obviously migrate from these extremes as winter approaches. As there is great variation in size there is also much diversity in the shape of their bill, due to modification for feeding from various flowers. The lance-billed hummingbird feeds from very deep bell shaped flowers, the sword-billed is adapted for feeding from the 6-in. long blossoms of datura trees, and the sickle-billed hummingbird is modified for feeding from flowers having verticle calyxes. The long tailed species are perhaps the most impressive. Several species such as the train-bearers, longtailed sylphs and the Jamaican streamer-tail have elongated central tail feathers almost twice the body length.

The Sunbirds

As a family the sunbirds are without doubt the most colourful of the nectar feeders, and take the place in the Old World of the hummingbirds. The East African malachite sunbird at 10 in. long is the largest species, and the Van Hasselts sunbird from south-east Asia is one of the smallest, being only $3\frac{1}{2}$ in. long.

The genus aethopygia is the most colourful and contains such locally common but seldom available species as the crimson, scarlet and Mrs. Gould's sunbirds. The males also have long tails with elongated central tail feathers. Sunbirds feed mainly at flowers, taking nectar and pollen and the small insects attracted to them. In areas where there is a definite seasonal variation in rainfall they are forced to make local migrations, or feed solely upon insects during the dry season when flowers are virtually non-existent.

VAN HASSELT'S
SUNBIRD

SCARLET
SUNBIRD

In captivity the moulting period is a time of great stress for
sunbirds, and some species e.g. the beautiful sunbird, have a
particularly hard time. They vary in temperament but generally the wedge-tailed species are less aggressive than those with
long tails. They are more insectivorous in the wild state than
is often thought, and many species are adept at catching insects
in flight. The larger species such as the tacazzi, malachite,
bronzy, etc. are suitable for housing with tanagers, pittas,

carlet Cock of the Rock. The outstanding member of any softbill collection however rare its
ompanions. Even though regularly imported it still commands a high price.

elow, Brown-hooded Kingfisher. An easily kept, inoffensive Kingfisher. It will thrive on live
od, strips of raw meat and small fish and is ideal for planted aviaries-conservatory or outdoor.
t should not be wintered out, however.

Princess Wood Nymph. An attractive Hummingbird from Ecuador, one of many unusual species imported annually into the British Isles. Their nutritional requirements have been the subject of research and controversy in recent years and suitable foods can now be purchased commercially.

Stork-billed Kingfisher. The most colourful of the larger Kingfishers this species has been found easy to maintain if provided with young mice as the bulk of its diet.

Woodland Kingfisher. Although this species often occurs in the vicinity of water it is a 'forest' Kingfisher and preys upon insects, small lizards and amphibians. It nests in holes in trees, often in the abandoned nests of Woodpeckers and Barbets.

Yellow-winged Honeycreeper. The most attractive and regularly available Honeycreeper. It will thrive on a basic diet of soft fruit and nectar, plus a good quality insectile mixture and a little live food.

Below: Blue-winged Siva. An insectivorous bird from South East Asia, it is frequently imported and retailed at a fairly low price. It can safely be housed with a community group of small softbills.

robin chats and other small-to-medium-sized softbills, but do not do well when kept with larger, non-aggressive species, unless housed in exceptionally large flights. The smaller sunbirds—the lesser double collared, Van Hasselts and purple-banded species, can be kept with zosterops, flower peckers, small flycatchers and similar sized softbills provided that sufficient space is available, and most important, sufficient feeding stations.

The cocks of several species e.g. the purple and beautiful sunbirds, assume a non-breeding plumage and as a result resemble the females for several months each year.

The Honeycreepers

The honeycreepers are a purely New World sub-family distributed throughout tropical and sub-tropical Central and South America, including the West Indies. Their tongues are adapted for obtaining nectar and pollen from flowers.

The cock birds are among the most colourful of softbills, vying with the sunbirds and hummingbirds, and are therefore much sought after as avicultural subjects. In comparison the hens are sombrely clad in soft shades of green and brown. The majority of honeycreepers are gregarious and are peaceful with both related species and other birds. They can be housed with any non-aggressive species of similar size or slightly larger. It is of course unwise to house small birds with much larger species unless in relatively large aviaries, as many are intimidated by mere size and this is reflected in every movement made by the larger birds.

The honeycreepers are ideal companions for small tanagers, euphonias and chlorophonias, and insectivorous species such as the minivets, wagtails and niltavas. The black-headed honeycreeper is an exception to the general rule, as the cocks are usually most aggressive to males of the same species and occasionally to other small birds.

The bananaquit and diglossas are also members of this sub-family, which is closely related to the tanagers. The bananaquit is a widely distributed species and is a common inhabitant of secondary growth and cultivated areas in the West Indies, where it has less fear of man than most birds.

The yellow-winged or red-legged honeycreeper moults after the breeding season and for some months assumes female-like colouration, this being known as the eclipse plumage. This species and the purple and black-headed honeycreepers are regularly offered by importers, but the scarlet-thighed, blue, yellow-bellied and yellow-collared species and the bananaquits and diglossas are seldom imported.

In their natural habitat the honeycreepers are active birds, moving in flocks through the forest canopy searching for flowers and insects, often in association with the smaller tanagers. Many species also frequent areas where the forest has been cleared and dense secondary growth flourishes, as this usually includes a variety of berry producing shrubs.

The Flowerpeckers

They are all small, plump birds with short wings and tail, and occupy a wide range of habitat—forest, secondary growth and cultivated land, from India eastwards to New Guinea and Australia, and northwards to the Philippines. They are seldom available to aviculture even though many species are rather common in the wild. The males of several species are very colourful, in particular the crimson-breasted flowerpecker of Malaysia and Indonesia, which is blue above and yellow below and has a bright crimson crown and breast spot.

The flowerpeckers most frequently offered by exporters are the scarlet-backed and orange-bellied species, which are both widespread throughout south-east Asia, but unless shipped with great care they are rarely good travellers. There is also a dearth of exporters in that area who are prepared to bother with such delicate birds. Although they are said to congregate in large numbers in flowering and fruiting trees they are apparently not gregarious in the wild. In captivity they resemble the hummingbirds in their aggressiveness towards their own kind, but it has proved possible to house a small group of flowerpeckers together for a considerable time. When roosting they cluster together like the colies and zosterops. They are suitable companions for sunbirds, honeycreepers, manakins, small tanagers and flycatchers.

Although nectar forms a large part of their diet, they should not have an ad lib supply available throughout the day or they will consume little else. It appears to suit their digestive system more if they are forced to eat fruit for the first part of the morning before nectar is provided. The flowerpeckers are certainly not as hardy as the majority of the nectivorous softbills and are most susceptible to a sudden drop in temperature.

SCARLET BACKED
FLOWERPECKER

The White Eyes

White eyes are the hardiest, cheapest and most readily available of the nectar feeders, and are ideal for the beginner. Their nectar requirements are less than the other families within this group, and they have in fact been kept on a diet of fruit and insects only. There is no denying however, that they thrive on a diet which includes nectar.

They are widespread over the three zoogeographical regions of the Old World—the Ethiopian, Oriental and Australasian regions, but the Indian species are the ones most frequently imported. They are purely arboreal, ranging from mangrove swamps and montane forest to cultivated areas where they do a lot of damage to soft fruits.

There are 85 species and many sub-species of white eyes, but they differ mainly in size and the extent of the eye ring. Their size varies from $2\frac{1}{2}$ in. to 5 in. and their plumage is green above and yellowish-grey below. Their beaks are short and slightly decurved and they have the brush tongues typical of many nectar eaters. They are particularly destructive to small-leaved plants as they remove buds and shoots.

The Honeyeaters and Sugarbirds

Under the most recent system of classification the 2 species of South African sugarbird are included with the Australasian honeyeaters. They are alike in many respects but mainly in the structure of the tongue, which has a brush tip but is also grooved. Neither of the sugarbirds—the cape or Gurneys, both of which are fairly common in the wild—are imported with any regularity. This may be because they are not brightly coloured, being shades of brown and grey with bright yellow under-tail coverts, yet what they lack in colour they make up for in tail length, which in the male cape sugarbird can be 12 in. long.

The honeyeaters are less frequently available to aviculturists as they are restricted to the Australasian region, and in Australia, New Guinea and Papua are protected and their exportation prohibited. A few are occasionally available from West Irian, formerly Dutch New Guinea. Before the ban was imposed the most frequently seen species were the blue-faced honeyeater and the New Guinea friar bird. They are gregarious birds, and in addition to nectar feed upon berries and fruit and are therefore unwelcome in the fruit growing areas of Australia.

They show extensive variation of size and bill form, and there are honeyeaters which resemble thrushes, warblers, flycatchers and even sunbirds. They are found in practically every type of arboreal habitat.

The Hawaiian Honeycreepers
The Hawaiian honeycreepers are not related to the New World honeycreepers (the Coerebinae), but form a distinct family of birds endemic to the Hawaiian Islands, where many diverse forms have evolved. This adaptive radiation or filling of ecological niches where there is no competition from other families of birds, has resulted in some species becoming adapted for cracking seeds, others take the place of the truly insectivorous birds and the members of the drepanidae sub-family are the nectar feeders. These birds are strictly protected as they are as important for evolutionary studies as Darwin's finches of the Galapagos Islands. Many of the known species are already extinct.

The Frugivorous Softbills

The Fruit Pigeons

The fruit pigeons are far more deserving of a place in aviculture than they are normally given, as they are among the most colourful of softbilled birds and are relatively easy to maintain. They are usually avoided because of their rather prolific, soft droppings, and sedentary habits. They are not suitable subjects for small cages and should be housed in aviaries or flights, where there is less chance of them being soiled by fruit and droppings. They are ideal for large planted aviaries and can be housed with practically any non-aggressive softbills, even much smaller species, as they are very peaceful birds. When attempting to nest, however, they are likely to be aggressive towards birds of the same species. Because of their inoffensiveness the smaller fruit doves should not be housed with such normally aggressive medium sized softbills as the white-crested jay thrush, coleto mynah and long-tailed glossy starling, particularly if these birds are given the opportunity of nesting.

Fruit pigeons are basically green birds, but in many cases this colour is brightened with red and yellow feathering, and they are characterised by their short fleshy legs and skin extension on either side of their toes. Their bills are soft and weak, but as they have a very large gape they are capable of swallowing large whole fruits. The imperial fruit pigeons, the largest members of the sub-family, are seldom seen in captivity, possibly as they are rather dull birds with mainly dark green, grey and chestnut feathering. The fruit doves are smaller but are by far the most colourful of all the pigeons, and although they are therefore the most sought after fruit eating pigeons, like so many birds from south-east Asia and the south-west Pacific islands they are difficult to obtain. The species from further north, in the Philippine Islands, are occasionally offered on the bird market and include the yellow-breasted fruit dove, Merrills fruit dove and the amethyst brown fruit dove.

The green fruit pigeons are regularly available, and the thick-billed, pompadour and orange-breasted green pigeons are the most readily available species.

In captivity the fruit pigeons seem loathe to bathe, and because of their arboreal habits are obviously accustomed to bathing in the rain or amongst wet foliage. Unless they are kept outdoors they should be sprayed regularly. Their reluctance to indulge in any exercise other than flying from perch to feeding dish often results in an over-fat condition, unless their food intake is carefully regulated. In addition it is a good idea to place their feeding dishes on the floor rather than on a stand.

The Touracos

Like practically all fruit-eating birds the touracos are entirely arboreal, and are such active and agile birds amongst the trees, that it is a natural outcome for them to have become the most frequently kept frugivorous birds. They are mostly birds of predominantly green plumage, with bluish-violet tail feathers and wing coverts and crimson remiges. The main difference between species is in the ornamentation of the head, the purple-crested touraco having a short rounded crest of purple feathers, the Knysna touraco having a long upright crest pencilled with white and the Schalows a long pointed green crest.

The members of the genus musophaga have blackish-violet plumage and very colourful head markings, which, in the violet plantain-eater take the form of a broad frontal shield of bright yellow, red rimmed eyes, a white mark below the eye and brick red colouring on the head. The louries or go-away birds are a complete contrast as far as colouration is concerned, being shades of grey and white, although they are crested. The

South African grey lourie is the most commonly seen species in captivity but none of the louries enjoys the popularity of the touracos or plantain-eaters.

The rare great blue touraco has recently become more readily obtainable, but still commands a very high price. It is much larger than the other touracos, being 30 in. long compared with their average of 20 in.

KNYSNA
TOURACO

Touracos are found only in Africa, and only where there are sufficient trees, ranging from the scattered trees of the South African veldt to the gallery forests of East Africa, and throughout the primaeval forests of Central and West Africa. If given sufficient space, they do well in groups but they must be introduced into new quarters together. Well-established single birds or pairs infrequently tolerate the introduction of birds of the same species into their territory. Also, the difficulty in sexing these birds often results in fighting and injury. On the other hand mated pairs are usually inseparable.

The touracos are ideal companions for the larger softbills— fruit pigeons, hornbills, toucans etc., in large community aviaries, as they provide the activity often lacking in the other

Black-headed Honeycreeper. The most aggressive of the Honeycreepers, particularly against individuals of the same species, and it is seldom possible to keep more than one pair per aviary however sizeable it may be. Their short beaks signify a basically insectivorous diet and they have been maintained without nectar.

Below, Yellow-throated Longclaw. An East African Pipit with rather a nervous disposition. It is mainly terrestrial and is of course highly insectivorous.

Black-fronted Bush-Shrike. A polymorphic species – having several colour phases. It is relate
to the Shrikes and is of course highly insectivorous. In captivity it must have a high protei
replacement mixture and plenty of live food.

Below, D'Arnauds Barbet. An attractive inexpensive African species which can share an aviar
with small Tanagers, Honeycreepers and similar softbills without fear. Like all Barbets the
tunnel, but they should be kept over a natural floor as they dig vertically into the soil.

species. Their nests are similar to the pigeons, and they are best provided with a shallow basket or wire platform to act as a base for the flimsy collection of twigs.

The Mousebirds

The mousebirds belong to a family of birds restricted to the Ethiopian region, and are characterised by powerful curved beaks and sharp claws. Another unusual feature is that the outer toes can be directed both forwards and backwards, an ideal adaptation for birds which creep about in bushes and cling to perches from all angles, their preferred position being vertically at right angles to the perch. Their name obviously originated from their creeping habits and from their soft grey colouring which is very mouse-like. They are regarded as vermin by the South African fruit growers because of the damage they do in the soft fruit orchards. They are not averse to taking animal food when an opportunity presents itself, and have been known to destroy the nests of other birds and carry off the neslings.

Mousebirds, or colies as they are also known, are very sociable birds and are normally encountered in small parties. When roosting they cluster together, often hanging belly to belly. They are crested and have long tails, and the few species in the family differ mainly in their facial or back colour, the white-backed, chestnut-backed, red-faced and white-headed having common names which are self descriptive. They are best housed in aviaries where there is ample dense cover such as privets or hawthorn bushes in which they can clamber about.

It is surprising that they are not more frequently imported as in parts of their range they are said to be exceedingly common. Neither are they aggressive birds, and are suitable companions for tanagers, niltavas and small barbets.

The Barbets

Most of the members of the barbet family are omnivorous in their feeding habits and are therefore included in chapter 11, together with some basic notes on the family.

A few species appear to be solely vegetarian in diet, according to such reliable observers as Alexander Skutch and T. H. Harrisson. The wild diet of the prong-billed barbet of Central America has been exhaustively studied by Skutch and consists of flowers, fruit and berries—a typical frugivorous diet. This also applies to several Oriental region barbets, in particular the gold-whiskered and golden-naped species, which have only been recorded as eating fruit and berries.

One African species—the yellow-fronted barbet of Tanganyika and Rhodesia, has only been recorded as eating fruit, particularly wild figs.

Unfortunately none of these barbets is readily available to aviculture.

The Waxwings

There are only three species of waxwings, but they are all regarded as choice avicultural exhibits as they are such beautiful birds, characterised by their soft vinaceous brown and grey plumage. The black tail is tipped with yellow and the secondary flight feathers with red "sealing wax" droplets. The bohemian waxwing of the Holarctic region is slightly larger and more colourful than the North American cedar waxwing, and the Japanese species has a pink tipped tail.

They are rather inactive birds in captivity in cages and indoor flights, and are best housed in outdoor aviaries. They quickly adapt to these conditions and can be kept with the smallest softbills without fear.

In the wild state they are gregarious and flock to trees laden with berries, which form the bulk of their diet. Insects are also taken occasionally, but more frequently when the waxwings are rearing their young.

The Omnivorous Softbills

The Hornbills

The hornbills are impressive birds, but the majority of species are more suitable for exhibition in zoological gardens unless large flights can be provided for them. Many are very aggressive and potentially dangerous to other birds, and the larger species—the rhinoceros, helmeted and great Indian hornbills, should never be housed with other softbilled birds. The medium sized hornbills—the pied, tarictic and crested species being typical examples, should only be kept with such softbills as toucans, jays and the large fruit pigeons and similar birds which are able to take care of themselves. It is most important however that ample space should be available to mixed collections such as these. The red-billed, yellow-billed, Monteiros, crowned and other small species of hornbills can normally be housed with much smaller species of softbills. Glossy starlings, kiskadee flycatchers and grackles would be suitable companions for them, but again, only if a large flight can be provided.

The hornbills have perhaps the most highly evolved nesting habits of all the softbilled birds. All the omnivorous species nest in holes and the entrance hole to the nest cavity is almost completely sealed with a mixture of mud, saliva, droppings and plant fibre. The cock bird feeds the hen through the narrow slit left open. The incubation period varies from about 30 days for the tockus species to 50 days for the bycanistes species. It has been observed that both the male and female red-billed hornbill share the task of sealing the nest entrance until the hen can just squeeze in. Five eggs are then laid at daily intervals after which the female is sealed in, both birds again assisting.

Although it might be expected that the eggs would be laid upon the rotten wood provided, this was not so and the nest box was filled to within a few inches of the top with palm fronds, leaves and grass. On the first nesting occasion the hen remained in the box for 17 weeks and was fed untiringly throughout, but the eggs proved to be infertile. At the second attempt the incubation period was approximately 34 days after which both hen and chicks remained in the nest box for 38 days. When the hen emerged the opening was re-sealed by the young, but they remained in the nest for only a further 6 days. The young birds differed from their parents in bill size only. On both occasions the hen was in excellent condition and fully feathered when she emerged. Although many smaller species of birds were housed in the same flight, the adult hornbills were only aggressive towards a tarictic hornbill during the nesting period.

Hornbills are restricted to the Ethiopian and oriental regions, and with the exception of the African ground hornbills are mainly arboreal. The species inhabiting tree studded savanna and bush country are more insectivorous and feed on the ground.

The Barbets

Most of the barbets are omnivorous in their feeding habits and include the species most frequently available to the aviculturist. The blue-throated barbet, like the majority of Asian species, is a green plumaged bird with crimson crown and pale blue throat and neck. It is regularly imported from India and is a relatively hardy bird. Occasionally imported from the same country is the coppersmith barbet, but this is not such a hardy species and can be aggressive towards smaller birds. The much larger lineated green barbet is also offered by the Indian exporters, but is a sombre bird and is not a favourite.

The blue-throated and lineated barbets can be wintered out if provided with a heated shelter, but the more delicate coppersmith is best housed indoors throughout the winter months.

Nest boxes should always be provided for barbets, even if

only a single bird is kept, as they normally roost in holes. If possible a block of partly rotten wood should be suspended from the highest point of the aviary as they prefer to make their own nest cavities.

COPPERSMITH BARBET

Several African species are occasionally available and include the small inoffensive D'Arnauds barbet and the larger black and red double-toothed barbet, both from East Africa. The African and New World barbets are the most colourful, and of the latter the toucan barbet, black-spotted barbet and red-headed barbet are sometimes imported, but never with the frequency of the Indian species.

Like most of the members of the order piciformes the barbets are arboreal, ranging from tropical forest to tree-studded grassland. A few species, e.g. the D'Arnauds and yellow-breasted barbets, prefer to nest in banks like the bee-eaters and are adept at burrowing. When given the opportunity D'Arnauds barbets will ignore tree stumps and burrow into the soil, often vertically.

The Toucans

Toucans, like the hornbills, are more suited to aviary, large flight or conservatory existence and do not do well in small cages where they are restricted to bouncing from perch to perch. They are certainly the most impressive softbills and are probably the most well known due to the publicity attracted by their colourful, enlarged bills. They should not be housed with other softbilled birds unless considerable space is available for them. The size of their companions will depend mainly upon the height of their quarters as well as the floor area, as toucans seek the highest branches for perching and seldom venture lower except to feed.

The smaller aracaris are also aggressive birds and should not be housed with small inoffensive softbills, whereas the toucanets are usually peaceful and are suitable for medium sized aviaries in company with glossy starlings, jays etc.

The toucans inhabiting the north-west corner of South America and Central America are the most frequently available on the bird market; the sulphur-breasted toucan, green toucanet and banded aracari being regularly imported and reasonably priced. Because of the habit of some exporters of sending several toucans in one shipping crate many cases of blindness occur as the birds jab constantly at each other with their soiled bills.

If toucans arrive from abroad in a weakened condition, they should on no account be force-fed. Although nestling toucans are force-fed when they are hand reared, wild caught adults seldom survive such treatment, and are best placed in a warm room, provided with water and a wide choice of food and left completely alone.

They are gregarious birds and often when one is shot by hunters the other members of the group respond to the cries of the wounded bird and mob the hunters. The mountain toucans of the Andes have been offered by importers in recent years, but never in any number. Like all "new" species when first imported they command high prices. They are of course more suited to outdoor flights than to humid conditions.

The American Trogons

The trogons of tropical Central and South America are brilliantly coloured birds, the adult males of several species being metallic green or violet with a bright red or pink breast. The mainly insectivorous Asiatic species are generally less brightly plumaged.

The resplendent trogon or quetzal is the most frequently exhibited trogon in zoological gardens, and is certainly the most spectacular of the New World trogons. Throughout their range the quetzals are restricted to the "cloud" forests, usually between 4,000 and 9,600 ft. where it is cool and very damp. They nest in holes, often enlarging old woodpecker nests, and as far as is known for the first few days raise their young upon insects only, most of which are caught on the wing. Fruits and berries form the bulk of the adult bird's diet, and these are mainly plucked from trees whilst they are hovering. When provided with a complete diet and suitable conditions quetzals have lived for many years in captivity, although it was not until 1937 that the first specimens were successfully exported from Central America, having been hand-reared by von Hagen.

Several species of trogons are offered by the bird exporters of Ecuador. Of these the violaceous trogon is a beautiful bird, having bluish-green upperparts, dark blue head and upper breast and the remaining underparts organge. The white-tailed trogon is a slightly larger but very similar bird.

Trogons are generally rather sluggish birds in their natural habitat, yet in captivity tend to be nervous and easily startled.

The Broadbills

Broadbills are seldom available and only one species, the lesser green, is offered with any regularity. The many other members of this handsome family, although common in the wild, are almost without exception never seen in bird collections. Apart from several species of two genera endemic to Africa they are otherwise Asiatic, occurring throughout the Oriental zoogeographic region. Like the trogons the broadbills can also be sub-divided into omnivorous species and purely insectivorous species. No doubt the relatively frequent availability of the lesser green broadbill is due to its omnivorous feeding habits, as a result of which it is easier to establish. Although this species would probably survive for short periods upon fruit alone, they will not do well unless provided with a good insectile mixture and live food.

Other omnivorous species are Whitehead's broadbill and Hose's broadbill, but both are endemic to Borneo, an island from which few birds reach aviculturists.

The omnivorous broadbills are gregarious and are usually most active at dawn and dusk. They are arboreal and are capable of taking insects from leaves in an ungainly manner. They quickly adjust to captivity and become quite tame, particularly if mealworms are offered.

The lesser green broadbills are completely harmless towards other softbilled birds and can be housed with honeycreepers, tanagers, chats, reedlings etc.

The Manakins
The superb or blue-backed manakin is the only species available to aviculturists with any frequency, and it follows that this and possibly the similar long-tailed manakin from Central America are the easiest species to establish. They are gregarious birds and are denizens of the rain forest undergrowth, ranging from Mexico to Argentina, where, like the trogons, they feed upon berries plucked in flight and insects. Many species frequent secondary growth, and in Trinidad the black and white manakin and golden-headed manakin are exceedingly common in this type of vegetation.

Manakins are difficult birds to establish and in captivity the moulting period seems to place much more stress upon them than on other birds. This is no doubt due to a dietary deficiency. The blue-backed and long-tailed manakins are never too interested in mealworms and normally will only accept maggots if forced to through lack of other foods. Their feeding should be carefully regulated as they will ignore insectile mixtures and feed solely upon fruit if given the opportunity. Also, if nectar is available ad lib for their companions the manakins are likely to consume large quantities, to the detriment of their digestive systems. Nectar should therefore be offered in limited amounts and the insectile mixture should be incorporated with the diced fruit in order that it cannot be avoided.

As they are gregarious birds manakins can be kept in groups, if such numbers are ever available, and in fact thrive when several are housed together, when signs of aggression have been non-evident. They are ideal subjects for heated, planted aviaries, and although they probably have been wintered out it is a risk which not many aviculturists are prepared to take.

The manakins are active birds in captivity and in addition to their bright colouration have a very interesting and complicated display.

The Cotingas
Two species of cotinga are readily available and until recent years commanded high prices, but the bird market has recently reached almost saturation point with both the orange and scarlet cocks of the rock, and their prices have dropped accordingly. They are no longer the prerogative of the specialist bird importer and are now freely obtained by many animal dealers. In addition they are hardy species and are long-lived in aviculture.

The other cotingas are not as readily available although the organge-breasted, green and black, scaled and cherry-throated species are sometimes included on dealers' lists. They have been regarded in the past as delicate birds, but this is not so as they are no more trouble than most of the tanagers. Like many South American birds they often arrive in this country heavily infested with mite, but once these are eradicated and the birds established they thrive. Unlike the cocks of the rock, which are well known for their aggressive tendencies, the smaller cotingas mentioned above are peaceful birds and can be housed with small softbills.

Not all the cotingas are brightly coloured. The mourners, becards, attilas and pihas are mainly grey and black, and are therefore of little interest to most softbill enthusiasts. Also included in the cotinga family are the bellbirds, umbrella birds and fruit crows, but only the bare-throated bellbird is regularly offered by importers. They are mainly frugivorous and have very wide gapes, and several species have been exhibited in zoological gardens, the New York Zoo having had the honour of exhibiting for the first time both the long-wattled and eastern umbrella birds. In this collection also, the rare mossy-throated bellbird of Trinidad's forested Northern Range and mainland South America made its first public appearance. The other species of bellbird—the single wattled, which has a fleshy upstanding process arising from the upper mandible, and the three wattled, are extremely rare birds.

The fruit crows are also rare in captivity and are seldom represented even in large zoo collections. The reason for their scarcity, and other cotingas too, is because the majority of species frequent the tree canopy, which in the tropical rain forests of the New World can be 150 ft. above ground. Consequently they are difficult to trap, particularly as many are localised and are found only in inaccessible areas. Although the cocks of the rock are also localised they occur in the lower levels of the forest and nest on rocky outcrops in small colonies, fixing their nests to rock ledges. In the more accessible regions the fledgelings are at the mercy of both the native tribes and professional bird trappers, resulting in the cocks of the rock being the most common cotingas in captivity. In the Pacaraima Mountains on the Brazilian border of Guyana the Amerindians are well aware of the existence of the nesting sites of the orange cock of the rock, and in February and March many young birds are taken to be handreared.

The Bulbuls

Several Indian bulbuls are regularly imported and are ideal subjects for the novice softbill keeper. The red-vented, white-cheeked and red-eared are the most frequently offered species and are hardy birds which are well able to withstand low temperatures if properly acclimatised. They are also peaceful and are suitable for mixed collections of softbilled birds in garden aviaries. The black-crested yellow bulbul and the yellow-vented bulbul are also mildly dispositioned.

Bulbuls are restricted to the Old World, but the African species are seldom offered with the regularity of their Asiatic relatives, even though equally common in the wild. In their natural state they are truly omnivorous and feed upon whatever animal food is available from snails to cockroaches, and at least 2 species—the Philippine bulbul and the black-crested yellow bulbul are capable of catching insects on the wing. They also eat berries, seeds and flowers. They are found in almost every type of habitat from the semi-arid regions, e.g. the red-eyed bulbul of south-west Africa, to the tropical rain forest, e.g. the yellow-crowned bulbul of Malaysia; and from the town and garden dwelling yellow-vented bulbul to the secretive black and white bulbul, both of Malaysia.

The Leafbirds
There are 3 genera within the family of leafbirds, but only the members of 2 of these play an important part in aviculture. The chloropsis, or fruitsuckers as they are commonly known, are to be seen in practically every large collection of softbilled birds, while the fairy bluebirds are becoming more common on the bird market and are now offered at temptingly low prices too. The other genus iora, has some attractive members, clad mainly in yellow, green and white and resembling the chloropsis in size and shape, but with a straighter bill. Although they are as common as the chloropsis, and presumably more easily obtainable than the fairy bluebirds due to their habit of frequenting gardens and cultivated areas, they are seldom offered by bird dealers. This may be due to their more insectivorous nature, but they also occur in India from where many flycatchers and other purely insectivorous species are exported annually.

The chloropsis are attractive birds with their predominantly green plumage enlivened with black, orange or blue upon the face or throat. They are active, hardy and adaptable birds, and quickly become accustomed to captive conditions. In the wild their diet comprises approximately equal parts of fruit and insects, nectar also being taken. The gold-fronted chloropsis from India is the most readily available, but the other common species from that country—the Jerdons chloropsis, is never imported with the same regularity. In fact, the orange-bellied or Hardwicks chloropsis of Thailand and Malaysia is more often seen in collections. All chloropsis are likely to be pugnacious to smaller birds and among themselves, when they are in condition. Frequently a few additional mealworms added to the daily ration are sufficient to upset a previously harmonious relationship.

GOLD FRONTED
CHLOROPSIS

Fairy bluebirds are less aggressive but nevertheless should preferably be housed with softbills of similar size. The cock is a beautiful bird, the glossy black of the underparts contrasting with the iridescent ultramarine of the upperparts. The hen is a dull bluish-green. In the wild they are gregarious birds which congregate on fruiting trees in company with hornbills, fruit pigeons and lories. They have also been seen feeding upon insects and nectar. From all accounts they are very common and are frequently offered in large numbers by the bird exporters of Singapore.

The Tanagers

More tanagers are probably imported into the British Isles than any other softbilled bird, as many thousands arrive annually. They certainly deserve their popularity as the majority are very colourful, reasonably hardy and quick to accept their new conditions, and thrive on the standard fare offered to most softbills. There are a few species which are rather delicate and should not be exposed to temperatures below 45°F (7.2°C). Several members of genus tangara fall into this category and include the speckled, flame-faced, superb and yellow-crowned tanagers. Surprisingly, two other members of the same genus, the golden-masked or Mrs. Wilson's tanager and the silver-throated tanager, are amongst the hardiest of the

PARADISE TANAGER

tanagers and probably the commonest in aviculture.

The tanagers vary considerably in their habits. Some are solitary birds and are seen singly or in pairs, whereas others, mainly the canopy dwellers, are gregarious and travel in flocks in search of fruiting trees. In Guyana the silver-beaked tanager roosts singly or in small numbers in densely foliaged tall bushes, yet in southern Trinidad many hundreds have been observed roosting in reedbeds in the company of black-throated orioles.

The blue and palm tanagers and the migratory North American species of the genus piranga, e.g. the summer, western and hepatic tanagers, and the rhamphocelus species, e.g. the scarlet, scarlet-rumped and yellow-rumped tanagers, are the hardiest species and once acclimatised can be safely wintered out.

The smaller chlorophonias and euphonias are generally more delicate than the tanagers, and often do not travel well from their country of origin. The chlorophonias are rather stumpy, thickset birds of basically green plumage which is enhanced with blue or yellow about the head. The blue-crowned chlorophonia is the most commonly imported species, and both they and the euphonias are peaceful birds and can be housed with any non-aggressive softbills.

Several of the larger species of tanagers, particularly the magpie tanager and the giant mountain tanager are inclined to be pugnacious towards smaller birds.

The Old World Orioles

The family oriolidae is restricted to the Old World and many of the 28 species show the brilliant yellow and black associated with the orioles, and usually have a reddish coloured bill. Several Asiatic species are also predominantly black but crimson replaces the yellow. The maroon oriole of the Himalayas and the mountainous areas of Burma and Thailand is a striking bird in which glossy crimson-maroon is relieved by the black head and wings.

There are several species of black-headed oriole but the Malaysian is the most impressive. In this species the golden-yellow of the underparts is replaced with white streaked with black.

Within this family the females are generally duller or more streaked than the males. All the species are arboreal and vary their diet with insects and berries. In captivity they are hardy, long-lived and relatively peaceful, although they should not be housed with smaller birds. They make ideal companions for mynahs, tree pies, grackles etc.

The New World Orioles

The American orioles show more diversity than the preceding family and include the troupials, cowbirds, meadowlarks, caciques, oropendolas, grackles and American blackbirds. They are adapted for existence in a variety of habitat, ranging from the rusty blackbird which is found within the Arctic circle, to the terrestrial grassland species of middle North America, and southwards to the arboreal rain forest members. Most of the temperate region species migrate to the tropics during the winter months.

The troupials and marshbirds are the most frequently available of the New World orioles; the spot-chested oriole, Baltimore oriole, common hangnest and the red-breasted and yellow-headed marshbirds often being advertised by importers.

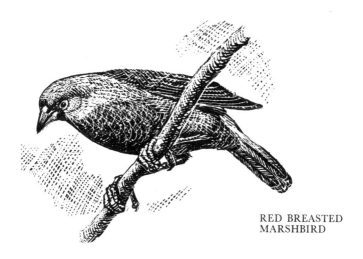

RED BREASTED
MARSHBIRD

Of the caciques and oropendolas the yellow-rumped cacique is sometimes imported, as are the large Central American waglers and montezuma oropendolas. They are polygamous birds and their nesting colonies often contain over 100 woven pendulous nests over 6 ft. long.

All the members of this family are easy to cater for and are long-lived, hardy and seldom aggressive to other birds. The yellowish-orange colouring of the orioles and the yellow-headed blackbirds is likely to fade in captivity and a colour holding or restoring agent should be added to the diet.

The Starlings

From the avicultural point of view the starlings are great favourites as they are easily catered for, are hardy and adaptable, and include some of the most colourful softbilled birds. With one or two exceptions they are the perfect example of the truly omnivorous bird. Their only disadvantage is that they are generally inclined to be aggressive, particularly when breeding. The greater hill mynah must be the most well known of all softbilled birds, but even more readily available and cheaper in price are the common mynah, bank mynah and Brahminy mynah. These are also Indian species but of little interest to the "pet" seeker, as they do not have the mimicking propensity of the hill mynahs.

Mynahs of more interest to the discerning aviculturist include the rare Rothchild's mynah which occurs only on the island of Bali, the coleto mynah of the Philippines and Dumonts mynah of New Guinea.

The starlings are well represented in Africa by the glossy starlings of which the superb glossy or spreo starling and the royal starling are the most beautiful, as their glossy black is enhanced with chestnut, white and yellow. The green, purple-headed and long-tailed glossy starlings are also attractive birds even though they are merely shades of glossy blue, purple and green. The wattled starlings and the violet-backed starlings, both East African species, are more insectivorous than the species already mentioned. Other interesting but seldom obtainable African species are the regal bristle-crowned starling, the magpie starling and the very beautiful splendid glossy starling.

Glossy starlings of the genus aplonis are also found in Malaysia, Indonesia, New Guinea and Polynesia, but seldom

range Ground Thrush. Terrestrial in habits, this species will make full use of the aviary floor,
often wasted in softbill collections. It may be aggressive to smaller ground-dwellers as it is
ighly territorial.

elow, Sulphur-breasted Toucan. The most frequently available, and most colourful of the
rge Toucans. This species should only be housed with large softbills such as Jays, Jay Thrushes
nd Fruit Pigeons. It has a definite need for animal protein.

Pileated Jay. A common South American Jay which should be housed with birds of equal size.
It needs ample roughage in the form of chicks and mice, plus a coarse insectile mixture and
little fruit.

Below, Necklaced Laughing Thrush. A frequently imported inexpensive species with very definite
aggressive tendencies. A positive menace to nesting birds, small, inoffensive and injured specimens.

reach these shores due to the paucity of bird collectors in those areas.

If starlings are housed in community aviaries their companions should be chosen with great care, as although several are peaceful birds, e.g. the violet-backed starling, the superb glossy starling and the common Indian mynah, many are very pugnacious, particularly if paired off and are attempting to nest. The coleto and Rothchild's mynahs, the Javan and greater hill mynahs and the long-tailed glossy starlings are noted for their aggressiveness, and should only be housed with jay thrushes, jays, aracaris and similar species which are capable of taking care of themselves.

Starlings are regular bathers and should always be provided with a large shallow dish of water. They are mainly hole nesters, one exception being the long-tailed starling of New Guinea which weaves long pendulous nests similar to the oropendolas.

The Song Babblers

Most of the babblers are insectivorous birds, but the members of the group identified as the song babblers are decidedly omnivorous, and include two birds which are beginner's softbills, because they are easy to maintain and normally do not present any dietary problems. One of these, the Pekin robin or red-billed leiothrix is the ideal bird for novice bird keepers. It is cheap, colourful and adapts quickly to cage life. The other "easy" species is the white-crested jay thrush, which is also reasonably priced and hardy, and although it is less colourful than the Pekin robin it is still a very conspicuous bird. It is, however, likely to be aggressive towards smaller birds. This also applies to several other species of jay thrushes, particularly the necklaced jay thrush.

Another member of this group is the silver-eared mesia, an attractive Asiatic species which is also easy to maintain. The small crested babblers of the genus yuhina are occasionally available, in particular the black-chinned yuhina. These and the ixulus which belong to the same genus are more difficult to keep than the other species in this group, and require a more refined diet. Like many of the species within the family muscicapidae they are sociable birds and occur in small flocks in the wild.

The Bowerbirds and Catbirds
Both the bowerbirds and related catbirds are restricted to the Australasian zoogeographical region, and with the exception of the species occurring in West Irian are unlikely to be available to aviculturists, or most zoological collections for many years, if at all.

The most unusual and well known feature of the bowerbirds is their habit of constructing bowers on the ground, which have no connection with their nest, as they are otherwise arboreal and nest in trees in the normal way. The bowers take several forms and are decorated with shells, coloured stones and fruit pulp.

All the species are fruit and insect feeders and rear their young during the season when most insects are on hand, in keeping with the majority of fruit-eating and omnivorous birds.

The satin and bowerbird is one of the few "tool users" of the bird world, as it uses a twig or piece of bark to daub a mixture of saliva and charcoal on to the bower.

The Birds of Paradise
Like the members of the preceding family the birds of paradise occurring in Australia, New Guinea and Papua are not available to the private aviculturist or to most zoological gardens. It is only the species inhabiting the western half of New Guinea, now controlled by Indonesia and known as West Irian, that are occasionally available at exorbitant prices. They are protected of course by political barriers rather than by concern for their perpetuation.

With few exceptions the longevity of birds of paradise exhibited in zoological gardens has never been very high, even though most specimens have been received as juveniles. The fact that males take several years to attain their adult plumage indicates a relatively long life span under natural conditions.

Sexual dimorphism is shown by all the birds of paradise except by the group of black species which include the manucodes and paradigallas.

Many birds of paradise have been housed in almost conservatory conditions whereas it is known that a number of species occur only in the mountainous regions of New Guinea above 5,000 ft., where it is both cool and damp. In the wild fruits and berries are the mainstay of all species, and this diet is varied with insects, small reptiles and amphibians. In captivity they thrive upon the standard omnivorous birds diet, which should be supplemented with roughage in the form of locusts and crickets for the smaller species and young mice and dissected day old chicks for the larger birds of paradise.

The greater bird of paradise still thrives in small numbers on the island of Little Tobago in the Caribbean, where the descendants of breeding stock released there early this century by Sir William Ingram are still holding their own, despite the devastation of a recent hurricane.

The Crows

The name "crow" is used in the general sense for all members of the family Corvidae, although the birds not included in the genus Corvus are commonly known as jays, tree pies, magpies, choughs etc., and within that genus rook, jackdaw and raven are accepted common names. With a few exceptions, such as the nutcrackers of the Nearctic and Palearctic regions which feed upon pine seeds and nuts, and the piapiac of West Africa which is mainly insectivorous, the members of the crow family are typically omnivorous, even to the extent of adding carrion to their very varied diet.

They are fearless and aggressive and have definite predatory tendencies, attacking and eating smaller birds, nestlings, eggs and small vertebrates. They should never be kept with small softbills, and in fact are best housed on their own or in the company of parrots or pheasants, although if the latter nested their eggs would be in jeopardy. The tree pies are less aggressive than the other members of the family and have been housed with other birds only half their size without trouble.

Neither the ravens, even the unusual African species—the white-necked, great-billed and fan-tailed, nor the typical crows are important in aviculture; whereas the jays and magpies are frequently seen in collections. Several American species are occasionally available and include the South American green jay, the attractive crested magpie jays of Central America and the stellers jay of North America, a handsome crested blue and black species.

With the exception of the Indian jays—the red-crowned and lanceolated jays, the Asiatic species are rare in captivity, which is a great pity as one, the loo-choo jay, is a splendid bird.

The most easily obtained corvids are the Himalayan blue magpie and the tree pie. Both are ideal for the novice softbill keeper as they are hardy and easy to maintain. The blue magpie however should not be trusted with small softbills.

TREE PIE

The Quail Doves

The New World quail doves and the following group, the ground doves of the Pacific islands, are not usually regarded as softbilled birds, yet they feed upon insects and fruit, are "aviary" birds and their young are altricial. They also include seeds, shoots and buds in their natural diet.

The quail doves are restricted to the sub-tropical and tropical forest zones from southern Mexico to Argentina, including the West Indies, and they spend most daylight hours on the ground but roost in trees at night. Many species are attractively coloured and are excellent for conservatory aviaries and outdoor flights. They should be provided with heat during the winter however, as they are not hardy birds and must be protected from cold winds and low temperatures.

The crested quail dove or mountain witch of Jamaica is a beautiful species which is becoming increasingly rare in the wild, but fortunately a number are bred annually in America. The mainland quail doves are in little danger of extinction due to the inaccessibility of most parts of their range, and are therefore safe for many years from the encroachment of civilisation. They are shot by the Amerindians for food, but this is a hazard which they have successfully weathered for years.

The Pacific Ground Pigeons

Several members of this group of softbills are commonly exhibited in zoological gardens and are kept by private aviculturists. The bleeding heart pigeon of the Philippines is the best known of these, and has for many years been a firm favourite in bird collections, having bred at the London Zoo as long ago as 1887. The Nicobar pigeon, a metallic green bird with slate grey head and wing feathers, and collar of greenish-bronze hackle plumes, is the only member of the group which extends its range to the Indian Ocean islands from which it has taken its name.

The crowned pigeons of New Guinea and its neighbouring islands are splendid birds, and are ideal for planted aviaries. There have however been instances of aggressive behaviour

towards smaller birds, and they are somewhat destructive to
low growing vegetation. Like the quail doves they are terrestrial
during the day, but roost and nest in trees. Unlike them
however they are hardy birds and can withstand low temperatures, although they should be given protection against frost.
They feed upon berries, insects, worms and seeds in the wild,
but the Nicobar pigeon is more granivorous than the others.
All too frequently their captive diet consists mainly of corn and
seed, and very little fruit or animal food, whereas the reverse
would be more suitable.

Other Pacific ground pigeons which have been available at
rare intervals in the past include the Bartletts pigeon, which is a
more spectacular version of the bleeding heart pigeon found
only on the island of Mindanao; and the pheasant pigeons of
the genus otidiphaps, which are restricted to the Papuan region.

Miscellaneous Omnivorous Softbills
Several families of omnivorous softbills have not been included
in the preceding pages as they have seldom been available to
aviculture in the past, and are hardly likely to be in the future.
The palm chat, found only on the islands of Hispaniola and
Gonave in the West Indies; and the wattlebirds of New
Zealand are typical examples. So too are the Australian
currawongs and apostlebirds, which are no longer available
because of the export ban on Australasian fauna.

The Insectivorous Softbills

The Sunbittern
Not only is the sunbittern the sole member of the family eurypygidae, it is also the only member of the order gruiformes —cranes, trumpeters, bustards etc., which can be included with the softbills, as it is an insect-eating aviary bird which has nidicolous young. Unlike the naked nestlings of the majority of softbilled birds, the newly hatched sunbittern chicks are covered with down and in this respect resemble the nidifugous young of the other species within the gruiformes, which leave the nest soon after hatching. Breedings at both the London and New York zoological gardens however have proved that the young are reared in the nest by the parents for 21 days before flying to the ground.

Sunbitterns are birds of the dense forest regions from Mexico to Brazil, and normally frequent water courses where they supplement their insect diet with small fish and crustaceans. They should not be housed with very small softbills, nor in confined areas with terrestrial species smaller than themselves.

The Cuckoos
The parasitic habits associated with the cuckoos are not characteristic of the cuculidae family as a whole, as there are many which are non-parasitic. The majority of parasitic species are commonly called cuckoos, whereas most non-parasitic species are known by other names, of which the malcohas, anis and coucals are examples.

Of the parasitic cuckoos the emerald, didric and klaas cuckoos are occasionally offered by East African exporters,

but the attractive pied crested cuckoo and the koel, both from
southern Asia, are more regularly available. The smaller species
are purely insectivorous and seem to favour caterpillars,
particularly hairy ones, whereas the larger cuckoos eat berries
and small vertebrates. The koel is probably the least insectivorous member of the family.

RED WINGED CRESTED
CUCKOO

   Cuckoos generally are characterised by their long tails which
are often graduated, and their relatively long wings, together
with a rather elongated body shape. The bill is fairly long and is
slightly decurved, and in the larger more carnivorous species
is very heavy. They are mainly solitary arboreal birds, the only
gregarious members of the family being the anis of tropical
America and the West Indies. These are non-parasitic and
construct nests of large masses of sticks. Like the magpie they
prefer to nest in tallish dense bushes, preferably thorny, about
10 ft. from the ground, but unlike them several females lay
their eggs in the same nest. They seek most of their insect food
from the ground, often following grazing cattle after the manner
of the cattle egret. They are hardly ever imported into the
British Isles, probably on account of their all-black plumage.

Scaly-feathered Ground Cuckoo. A non-parasitic species from the Philippine Islands, which is largely terrestrial, but roosts above ground. Although highly carnivorous it is not equipped to tear flesh and must be provided with food items that can be swallowed whole.

Dollar Bird. A typical aerial bird, showing the broad bill of the insect hawker, the long powerfu
wings for graceful flight and the poorly developed feet and legs. It naturally needs a great dea
of flying space in captivity.

Pygmy Kingfisher. An insectivorous African species only 4″ long, including its 1″ bill, it is the gem of the family. Thrives on shrimps, live food and small strips of meat.

White-collared Kingfisher. A widespread species in the old world tropics, it is also the commonest of the family in captivity, where it has bred several times. They are easy to maintain and are not aggressive towards other birds.

The Old World coucals are more colourful than the anis, being mainly black and white in body colouration, with coppery chestnut wings. Although basically insectivorous they are more carnivorous than the species already mentioned, and like the anis they construct large nests of sticks and grass, but several species, e.g. the black coucal and Flecks coucal, place their nests low down among tall grasses or dense undergrowth.

The malkohas are the most attractive members of the family, but like all birds native to Malaysia, Indonesia and the Philippines, they are seldom available due to the scarcity of trappers in those countries. They are by no means rare in their natural habitat, and from all accounts the Malaysian Raffles, lesser green-billed and chestnut-breasted malkohas are exceedingly common. A species which has been available several times in recent years is the scaly-crowned malkoha of the Philippines, which is probably the most colourful member of the group.

RAFFLES MALCOHA

The coucals, malkohas, anis and the larger parasitic cuckoos are inclined to be aggressive towards smaller birds, and should be housed only with softbills of similar size.

The North American roadrunners are considered to be carnivorous softbills and are therefore included in the chapter dealing with those birds.

The Old World Trogons

Unlike the American trogons the Asian species, with one exception, do not have metallic colouring, but are still attractively marked in shades of brown, pink and black. The few African species resemble their American counterparts.

They are almost entirely insectivorous, although a few species have been known to take berries and small fruits occasionally. Whilst they are capable of hawking insects, these are usually taken from leaves and tree trunks. They are arboreal and often crepuscular, and nest in hollow tree trunks and sometimes in termites' nests. Normally solitary birds they are sluggish and often confiding in the wild, and have a strong silent flight reminiscent of the owls.

None of the Old World trogons is regularly available and the number in captivity in the world, in both zoological gardens and private collections, is never more than a handful.

The Kingfishers

For a long time the kingfishers have been termed "forest" kingfishers or "fish-eating" kingfishers; the implication being that the forest species are purely insectivorous, and the fish-eaters entirely piscivorous, but it is not such a simple matter. Many of the fish-eating species also take insects and small vertebrates, and several of the insectivorous forest species also include fish in their diet.

Even grouping them as "burrowers" and "tree-nesters" is impractical as several species which burrow into river banks to nest, e.g. pygmy kingfisher and grey-hooded kingfisher, are in fact insectivorous species.

Generally speaking, the members of the sub-family cerylinae are the fishers and are therefore classed as carnivorous birds; and the daceloninae and alcedininae sub-families contain birds of both insectivorous and carnivorous habits. One member of the non-fishing group, the kookaburra, is also regarded as a carnivorous bird.

The insectivorous kingfishers are the most frequently kept although they are by no means common, even in the larger zoological gardens. Several African species are often available and include the pygmy kingfisher, the grey-hooded and brown-hooded kingfishers and the Senegal kingfisher. The Asiatic white-collared and white-breasted kingfishers are occasionally imported. All are easy to maintain and are peaceful towards other birds, but often aggressive towards the same species. As they need to dive into water to bathe they should be provided with a water dish or pool large enough to allow this.

The Todies

The 5 species of tody are restricted to the islands of the Greater Antilles in the West Indies; there being a representative on Cuba, Jamaica, Puerto Rico and 2 species on Hispaniola. They have recently been kept in the San Diego Zoo, but are never likely to be widely kept due to the difficulties involved in both acquiring and establishing them.

Todies are entirely insectivorous, and like practically all members of the order coraciiformes they nest in holes, which in their case are tunnels in banks similar to the bee-eaters and some kingfishers.

The Motmots

Motmots are perfect examples of the larger species of insectivorous softbills. Once established they are frequently long-lived, and when acclimatised are reasonably hardy. Often they do not travel well en-route to the British Isles, and it has been said that perhaps they suffer from shock as a result of close confinement in shipping cages. This seems hardly likely however for birds accustomed to tunnelling into banks, and nesting and roosting in a small hole in almost total darkness. Their poor travelling resistance is probably due more to their not having been properly established before shipment, as on several occasions shipping boxes have been found to contain only banana.

The motmots range from Mexico to the Matto Grosso of Brazil, where they inhabit only the forested regions. They are insectivorous and catch insects and other arthropods both in the air and on the ground. If housed in outdoor aviaries or in conservatories where the flooring consists of several feet of soil, they will almost certainly begin tunnelling. Often several tunnels are dug and are used for roosting.

The most impressive member of the family is the 18-in. long greater rufous motmot of western South America and Central America, but the species most readily available is the blue-crowned motmot which has cinnamon underparts, is olive-green above and has a shining turquoise crown.

Although they are not normally aggressive birds it is advisable not to house them with small softbills, as their heavy serrated bills could be used with great effect.

SITES FOR
BANK NESTERS   Bee-eaters, Kingfishers, Motmots etc.
                (a) OUT OF DOORS

RETAINING WALL OF BRICK OR CLAY. IMPACTED SOIL, HELD IN PLACE WITH IVY, GRASS, ETC.

(b) INDOORS

I in. THICK PLASTER CUT AWAY   NATURAL ROCKS WITH
TO SHOW WIRE MESH   BRICK RETAINING WALL

The Bee-eaters

Essentially hawking birds, the bee-eaters are seldom seen in
bird collections due to the difficulty of enticing them on to a
replacement diet, as they do not thrive solely upon mealworms
and maggots for any length of time. Also, it is a difficult task
to handrear nestlings.

They are best housed in glass fronted cages as this allows
the feeding of winged insects which would otherwise be
impractical in wire fronted cages. If housed outdoors during
the summer months insects can be attracted with meat or
syrup.

The bee-eaters are residents of the Old World, but they are
not restricted to the tropics as the European bee-eater, which
migrates to tropical Africa, has been known to breed in the
British Isles. Most species are gregarious and nest in colonies,
excavating tunnels in sandy banks. Although they are not
known to drink they are attracted to water, probably for the

insect life available over it, and likewise wheel in their thousands over grass-fires to feast on the insects disturbed.

Bee-eaters represented in captivity in recent years have
included the European, the bearded, the cinnamon-chested
and the little bee-eaters, but the most colourful species is

INDIAN ROLLER

undoubtedly the carmine bee-eater, which is extremely plentiful in East Africa. The smaller bee-eaters are not aggressive
and can be kept with similar sized softbills, but they tend to
intimidate smaller species such as flowerpeckers and small
sunbirds.

The Rollers

Rollers are easy to maintain and are long-lived once established,
and the task of meating them off is a relatively simple one,
although the broad-billed rollers can be a little troublesome.
The European roller and the Indian blue roller, which is
frequently offered by the Indian bird exporters, seem to be the
most adaptable to captive conditions and soon accept inanimate
foods. They are certainly not "cage birds" however and should
only be kept if they can be offered sufficient flying space, even
if they cannot indulge in their aerial acrobatics.

Like the bee-eaters they congregate at the scene of bush fires, but also catch insects on the ground as well as in flight. The broad-billed rollers have a less acrobatic flight than the other species, but have a much wider gape; whilst the gape of the Asiatic dollar bird is even wider.

In captivity they are frequently aggressive towards each other, even if not in condition, but seldom trouble other soft-billed birds only half their size. They tend however to attract the attention of the more aggressive softbills, as they do in fact in the wild. The lilac-breasted roller and the racquet-tailed roller, both tropical African species, are the most colourful and in addition they have elongated outer tail feathers, which are spatulate in the latter species.

The Hoopoes
One of the most easily recognised of all softbilled birds, the hoopoe occurs in the natural state over a wide area of the Old World, from Europe southwards to South Africa and eastwards to Sumatra. Most of the birds offered by Asiatic exporters are hand-reared specimens and are therefore well established, and quickly accept their new environment. Such birds have in fact bred several times in captivity.

They spend most of the daylight hours on the ground, probing the soil and rotting wood for worms, insect larvae and spiders, and even small snakes and frogs; but they nest in holes which are noted for their stench. This was not so in the captive breeding at the San Diego Zoo however, as the nests were clean and the female did not secrete the supposedly protective evil smelling fluid. Yet on the other hand an incubating female at the Winged World, Morecambe had a most unpleasant smell.

Hoopoes are not aggressive birds and have been kept with many smaller species of softbills including several species of tits, tanagers and honeycreepers.

The Wood Hoopoes
Although the wood hoopoes are closely related to the hoopoes they bear little resemblance to them. They are slimmer birds

and lack the crest and patterned plumage, and are mainly glossy green and purple. They are endemic to Africa, south of the Sahara, and like the hoopoe are found only in the more open bush country wherever there are ample trees. In their feeding habits they are more arboreal than the hoopoe and act more in the manner of the woodpeckers, probing for insects in bark and rotten tree trunks and using the tail as a support.

Generally they are seldom available to aviculture, but occasionally hand-reared specimens of the green wood hoopoe and the white-headed wood hoopoe are offered from East Africa. They are easy to cater for and accept the standard insectivorous diets very readily. They are peaceful birds and have been kept in rather over-crowded aviaries with pittas, chats and barbets without trouble. Enclosed nest boxes with a small entrance hole should always be provided for wood hoopoes, even if only a single bird is kept, as they prefer to roost in these and will also take refuge in them if alarmed.

The Jacamars
Like the bee-eaters the jacamars are difficult to meat-off, and are therefore best taken from the nest and hand-reared, but with the scarcity of South American bird trappers willing to undertake such a task they will always be rare in collections. Practically all their food is taken in the air, and they seem to prefer butterflies, which are beaten against a branch until the wings drop off.

They are beautiful birds, being mainly green above and rufous-brown below, with a white chin or breast; and the sexes are alike. They are birds of the forest clearings, paths and secondary growth, where there is space to survey their surroundings from an exposed branch, from where they make flights to catch passing insects.

The Oxpeckers
The oxpeckers or tickbirds are the only truly insectivorous members of the sturnidae family and they are restricted to the Ethiopian region. There are only 2 species—the red-billed

oxpecker and the less common yellow-billed oxpecker, and they feed almost entirely upon insects captured upon the backs of large mammals, both domestic and game species. Their diet of ticks and blood-sucking flies is also supplemented with a certain amount of tissue and blood taken when removing ticks from the hide.

Oxpeckers are relatively easy to maintain and have been provided with simulated beasts of hessian on a wire framework, but they are more suitable for zoo exhibition.

The Woodpeckers

Woodpeckers are both hardy and long-lived when established but they are by no means suitable for community aviaries as they are inclined to be aggressive towards smaller species of softbills and are a positive nuisance when other birds are attempting to nest.

GOLDEN BACKED
WOODPECKER

The vast forests of tropical South America contain a bewildering variety of woodpeckers, yet few species reach aviculturists; the majority of those that do hail from India, from where the golden-backed woodpecker is frequently exported.

Although it is generally assumed that all woodpeckers are arboreal, there are species which are virtually terrestrial, an example being the ground woodpecker of South Africa. They also show a great diversity of size, ranging from the diminutive piculets, in which the bill is insufficiently developed to drill holes, to the large almost extinct ivory-billed woodpecker of North America.

They are not widely kept due to their destructive habits where woodwork is concerned, yet they are normally well behaved if provided with logs or small tree trunks of well-dried wood.

Most species are purely insectivorous, but a few include fruit and nuts in their diet also, particularly the golden-fronted and Waglers woodpeckers. Many also eat ants, and the rufous woodpecker of India is said to live almost entirely upon ants, their eggs and larvae. It even nests in the ants' nest while they are still occupied. The majority of woodpeckers however nest in holes drilled into dead trees, or dead limbs of living specimens, and the piculets manage to excavate holes in very rotten wood. The ground-dwelling woodpeckers nest in holes in banks or in ground termites' mounds.

The Pittas

The pittas are the most beautiful of the terrestrial softbills, but they are seldom available. Until quite recently the Indian pitta and the hooded pitta were offered quite regularly by importers of Indian livestock, but the rarer species from Malaysia and the Philippine islands—the garnet pitta, red-breasted pitta and Steere's pitta are even less frequently available. This also applies to the Angola and green-breasted pittas of Africa.

Pittas are short, plump birds which roost on low branches but obtain all their food upon the ground, scratching amongst the leaves and soil like thrushes for worms, insects and small lizards. They nest upon the ground or in low tree forks, and the nest is said to be a large untidy globular affair of small twigs and grass.

GLOBULAR NESTERS—Pittas

Ample floor cover is essential for enticing
Pittas to rest in captivity.

It is unwise to house very small softbills with pittas, however
arboreal the former might be, as they will almost certainly be
attacked when they venture down to ground level to bathe or
feed. Due to their solitary nature pittas are often aggressive
towards each other if several are housed in an aviary with
limited floor space, as this will not allow them sufficient room
to establish their territories. They are certainly not difficult to
maintain from the feeding point of view, but they do not thrive
upon hard surfaces, either wet or dry. They should be kept on a
moistened mixture of peat and soil or leaf mould to keep their
feet in good condition. Should their toes dry and crack the
finest remedy is to place the birds upon a damp soil mixture,
rather than treat with oils or salves, which have little effect.

The Wrens

The birds which are commonly known as wrens are all members of the order passeriformes but belong to 3 unrelated families, the true wrens, the Australian fairy wrens and the New Zealand wrens.

The true wrens are restricted to the New World, with the exception of the common wren which occurs throughout the holarctic regions. They are very active birds, but lack colour and are therefore not highly regarded as avicultural subjects. What they lack in colour however they make up for in singing qualities, as they are great songsters which often become confiding and tame.

Even since the ban upon the exportation of Australian fauna the delightful fairy wrens have been offered by bird dealers with more frequency than the true wrens. They are beautiful little birds, clad in combinations of black, red, blue and white; whilst the related emu wrens are mainly brown coloured. Their woven domed nests have a side entrance, and they are apparently parasitised by several species of Australian cuckoos, which are considerably larger than the wrens.

The Mockingbirds

The mockingbirds are restricted to the New World, where they range from southern Canada almost to the tip of South America, including the West Indies. They therefore occur in a wide range of climatic conditions.

They are mainly terrestrial and are not brightly coloured; and their soft grey and brown plumage does not have many admirers. In addition they are aggressive birds which are more territorially conscious than most softbills. Like the wrens they are excellent songsters and mimics.

The blue and the blue and white mockingbirds are the species most likely to be seen in captivity, as they are the most colourful mockingbirds and are relatively peaceful. The catbirds, thrashers and tremblers belong to the same family as the mockingbirds, and with the exception of the catbirds many are confined to the West Indies.

All the mockingbirds obtain their food in the manner of the thrushes, searching amongst the soil, leaves and low scrub for the invertebrates which form the bulk of their diet. Several species are also said to eat berries.

The Flycatchers
The flycatchers are probably the most frequently imported insectivorous softbilled birds, several species being available regularly from India. These common species, such as the tickells and verditer flycatchers, are easy to maintain, and are relatively long-lived. The narcissus, white-browed blue and black naped blue flycatchers are occasionally imported but require more careful treatment than the common species. The paradise flycatchers often arrive in a weakened condition and are troublesome to "meat-off" and maintain in good condition for any length of time.

PARADISE FLYCATCHER

Of the niltavas, the beautiful rufous-bellied species is regularly imported and is easy to keep, whereas the other species are seldom available.

The majority of the flycatchers are peaceful birds although the paradise flycatchers are inclined to be aggressive towards smaller species. All have a penchant for bathing and care

should be taken in providing only a sufficient depth of water
for bathing in, as there are many cases on record of them
drowning, even in water dishes containing no more than 1 in. of
water. Their feathers appear to become water-logged very
quickly even though outwardly they may seem to be in good
condition and not dry or brittle.

Few flycatchers are available from Africa, and the puff-
backed and wattle-eyes species which have been imported in
recent years have proved to be far more difficult to establish
than the Asian flycatchers.

The Tyrant Flycatchers
Over 300 species of tyrant flycatchers occur in the New World,
yet only 1 of these, the kiskadee flycatcher, is available with
any regularity. Naturally it is a hardy bird and is not difficult
to cater for. In fact they are possibly the least discriminating of
the insectivorous softbills as they can be caught quite easily in
the simplest of traps baited with banana.

Very few of the other species of tyrant flycatchers—the water
tyrants, ground tyrants or kingbirds etc.—have ever been kept
in captivity, and there seems little likelihood of an improve-
ment in this situation.

Kiskadees are aggressive birds and small softbills and their
eggs and young are often included in the diet of the wild bird.
Their companions in captivity should therefore be chosen with
care.

The Cuckoo Shrikes and Minivets
The family campephagidae can be divided into 2 distinct
groups, the dull cuckoo shrikes and the colourful minivets. The
cuckoo shrikes are not important in aviculture, although many
are common in the wild, even in India where bird trapping and
exporting is so widespread. In fact, the large cuckoo shrike and
the black-headed cuckoo shrike are frequently offered by
Indian exporters, but very seldom appear on British dealers'
lists, although the more insectivorous swallow shrike is sometimes offered.

The beautiful minivets are purely insectivorous and are eagerly snapped-up by bird keepers whenever they are imported. Unfortunately they are seldom good travellers and many do not survive the journey from India. They are arboreal birds and are decidedly gregarious, moving through jungle and secondary growth in flocks, searching for insects and caterpillars. They show sexual dimorphism, the males of most species being red and black, and the females orange and grey. The minivets are peaceful birds and can be housed with any similar sized non-aggressive softbills.

The Wagtails and Longclaws

The wagtails, longclaws and the pipits all belong to the family motacillidae. They are mainly terrestrial birds and the pipits and longclaws inhabit open grassland or savanna country; whereas the wagtails are seldom found far from water and frequent rocky streams, marshes and paddy fields.

The wagtails are a rather confusing group of birds, as there are only 7 species in the genus motacilla, but there are many geographical races and sub-species. In addition several of the summer dwelling Palaearctic species migrate southwards to winter in warmer climes. They are ideal avicultural subjects and several species are regularly offered for sale, particularly by importers of Indian birds. The Indian and European races of the yellow and the white wagtails are the most commonly available species, together with the pied wagtail. They are all easy to maintain and are not aggressive towards other birds.

The pipits are of little interest aviculturally, but the longclaws have been imported several times in recent years. The most attractive species is the pink-throated longclaw of southeast Africa, but it is the yellow-throated longclaw from East Africa which can be seen in several of the larger bird collections. As their name suggests they are characterised by their extremely long claws, the hind claw being over $1\frac{1}{2}$ in. in length, an adaptation for living in swampy grassland. They normally roost several feet from the ground however, perching in a very ungainly manner.

While longclaws thrive on the standard insectivorous bird diet they should be kept upon a moist soil and peat mixture to avoid foot troubles. Unlike the wagtails, which normally soon settle down in aviaries and become quite tame, the longclaws are very nervous, retiring birds and require careful handling.

The Shrikes
The family laniidae embraces the true shrikes, the bush shrikes and the helmet shrikes, and although there are many species within the family it is probably the least represented of softbill groups, even in the largest collections. The helmet shrikes are purely insectivorous, but the shrikes and bush shrikes can be roughly divided into 2 groups; firstly those which are mainly insectivorous and secondly those which favour food items and take young mice, lizards, birds etc. The latter group is included with the carnivorous softbills in chapter 13.

Most shrikes are aggressive birds and should not be kept with smaller species of softbills. They are well known for their habit of impaling their prey upon thorns, but this habit is not characteristic of the family as a whole. Common to all species is the strong hooked bill, strong feet and sharp claws, all being adaptations for seizing, holding and tearing their prey. Several species catch insects in the air, although the normal method is to take their food from the ground. At least one species, the white-crowned shrike, is adept at catching large insects in flight in its feet.

Many of the insectivorous shrikes are very colourful, but they are seldom available. The crimson-breasted shrike of south-west Africa is a gorgeous bird, but unfortunately inhabits an area devoid of bird trappers. Doherty's bush shrike, black-fronted bush shrike and the straight-crested helmet shrike are occasionally offered by East African exporters. The Indian dealers usually offer the widespread and common Asiatic species such as the common wood shrike, but these are rarely imported.

The Thrushes and their allies

The large family muscicapidae contains more widely kept insectivorous species than any other family, as it includes the thrushes, robins, chats, redstarts, shamas, babblers and many others. Most of the species are relatively easy to maintain and are favourites of many softbill keepers.

Several species of Asian thrushes are regularly offered by bird importers, and include the attractive blue-headed rock thrush, the similar but duller chestnut-bellied rock thrush and the orange-headed ground thrush. They are all peaceful towards smaller arboreal species, but the orange-headed ground thrush is likely to be aggressive towards small terrestrial birds. The larger blue whistling thrush should be kept only with medium sized softbills such as starlings, grackles and motmots. Rarer species of ground thrushes become available from time to time, an example being the Abyssinian ground thrush.

Generally speaking the African species of true thrush are more arboreal than are the Asiatic thrushes, although they also seek their food upon the ground, but they are less colourful and are seldom imported. As a group, the chat thrushes are more terrestrial than the true thrushes, and accordingly have very slender legs. They are more colourful than the larger thrushes but do not have their singing qualities.

SHAMA

The chat thrush group contains many well known avicultural subjects, both hardy and delicate. The shama, an exception regarding singing powers, and the magpie robin, are both easy to maintain and are ideal birds for beginners. Their companions should be chosen with care, however, as they both have aggressive tendencies. Both the shama and magpie robin can be wintered out and thrive in low temperatures, provided sufficient exercise space is allowed.

MAGPIE ROBIN

Aggression is a common trait of the chat thrushes, due no doubt to their highly developed territorial instincts. Not only is it virtually impossible to keep more than a single pair of these birds in an aviary, but they also resent the introduction of other small species of unrelated softbilled birds, particularly terrestrial ones. The Asiatic blue chat and the rubythroat are perfect examples of the typically aggressive members of this group. The smaller species of chats, the bush chats and the redstarts are more insectivorous than the African robin chats, which are said to include berries and fruit in their wild diet.

With the exception of the blue chat and the rubythroat few Indian bush robins reach these shores. The beautiful golden bush robin is rarely imported. Of the redstarts only the white-capped species is imported in any numbers; the other common Indian species—the black, daurian and plumbeous redstarts are rarely seen.

The African robin chats are birds of rufous plumage and blue-grey wings, some species having black and white markings on the head. The Natal robin chat is the only species available with any regularity, although the snowy-headed and white-browed species are exhibited in a few of the larger bird collections.

The babblers are also included in the family muscicapidae, and of the insectivorous species the scimitar babblers are those most often kept. They are normally shy, elusive birds, but are quite hardy and relatively easy to maintain. In the wild they are said to include a few berries and small fruits in their diet.

SLATY HEADED
SCIMITAR BABBLER

They are gregarious and like so many flock birds the sexes are alike. Closely related to the scimitar babblers are the wren babblers, wren tits and tit babblers, but these birds are rarely available and are not important in aviculture.

The rockfowl or picathartes are now classed as babblers, and are considered to be closely related to the laughing thrushes. There are only 2 species, the grey-necked and the white-necked rockfowl, both endemic to West Africa, and the former has bright yellow on the head, and the latter pink. They are localised birds, with a wide expanse of territory separating the 2 species. The grey-necked rockfowl is only known to occur in Sierra Leone, Ghana and Togo, and the white-necked species is restricted to the Cameroons. They are active, intelligent birds and on the few occasions that they have been available have commanded a high price.

Neither the Old World warblers—the whitethroats, tailorbirds, kinglets etc.—which are now classified as a sub-family of the muscicapidae; nor the American wood warblers are of importance in aviculture. The American warblers actually belong to another family, the parulidae.

The Tits

The tropical tits are almost perfect subjects for indoor planted aviaries as they are colourful and very active, but they are inclined to be destructive to plant life. Several Indian species are frequently offered by exporters, particularly the green-backed tit, the Indian black tit and the attractive yellow-cheeked tit. The rare sultan tit, a beautiful crested yellow and black species, is always eagerly sought, but is offered with more frequency in North America than in the British Isles.

They are sociable birds which hunt for insects and their larvae among the foliage, often in the company of other insectivorous species. In the manner of the crows they are able to hold food with their feet, a modification which is useful for the species that include nut kernels in their diet, as they can hold the nut while hammering the shell open.

The sexes are alike in most species, which makes the formation of a pair a difficult task. Many tits are hole nesters, but the long-tailed tits and the penduline tits construct globular nests with a single small entrance hole. After the penduline tit has passed through, the hole closes.

The Nuthatches

Although there are 31 species of nuthatches, like the tits the only exotic species to have made any impression at all upon softbill keeping in Great Britain are Indian birds, the chestnut-bellied and the velvet-fronted. Unlike the tits the sexes are well defined in both species of nuthatches as the female velvet-fronted nuthatch lacks the conspicuous black stripe above the eye, which is present in the male; and in the female chestnut-bellied the colouring is paler and less well defined.

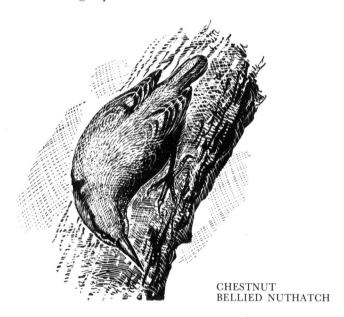

CHESTNUT
BELLIED NUTHATCH

The nuthatches should always be provided with ample vertical branches of a fairly thick diameter and with rough bark, or with wide strips of cork bark. They do not use the tail for support as do the woodpeckers, but are able to climb up and down tree trunks obliquely.

They are hole nesters and make use of natural holes or hollows, and when necessary reduce the size of the entrance with earth. The 2 species of rock nuthatches likewise seal-up the entrances of the rock cavities which are used for nesting, and in addition construct an entrance tube leading down into the nest hollow. In captivity the nuthatches are even more territorially conscious than the tits and it is unusual for more than one pair to be kept in an aviary for any length of time. They are not aggressive towards other small softbilled birds of similar size.

The Drongoes

The drongoes belong to a family of purely insectivorous softbills which are restricted to the Old World, and most strongly represented in the Oriental region. With two exceptions, which are slate-grey in colour, they are glossy black birds. Many species have crests and long forked or racquet tipped tails.

Only the Indian species, the common black drongo or king crow and the larger and more spectacular racquet-tailed drongo are available with any regularity. They are highly insectivorous and are therefore not the easiest of softbills to maintain. The racquet-tailed species is a good songster and mimic.

Although they are recorded as being extremely pugnacious towards larger, predatory birds in the wild, they do not molest smaller species which are said to take advantage of the protection they afford by nesting in the same bush.

The Malimbus Weavers

Within the ploceidae, a family of mainly seed-eating weavers, are included 10 species of black and red forest weavers, which are all insectivorous and belong to the genus malimbus. In addition a few members of the large genus ploceus feed solely upon insects.

Nowadays neither is important in aviculture due to its unavailability. The malimbus are confined to West Africa, from where it is becoming increasingly difficult to obtain the rarer and more delicate species of softbills. The insectivorous ploceus species, also from Africa, do not appear to have been imported for several years.

Miscellaneous Insectivorous Softbills

A whole host of insectivorous species have not been included in the preceding notes because of their unimportance as avicultural subjects, and their unavailability. The crepuscular and nocturnal species—the frogmouths, pottoos and nightjars, will probably never be seen with any regularity even in the largest bird collections, until perhaps "nocturnal bird houses" are constructed. The numerous species of South American antbirds, which include the ant pittas, ant thrushes, ant shrikes and ant wrens, are unlikely to appear on the bird market whilst the tanagers, which are easier to catch and maintain, are in such demand. In fact, the few connoisseur bird collectors such as Charles Cordier, are probably the only trappers who would go out purely to collect antbirds.

Birds restricted to countries which have seen their fauna decimated over the years, and have at last instituted protective measures, are seldom likely to be available in the future. This applies to the island of Madagascar, the home of those interesting birds the cuckoo roller and the vanga; and to Australia where the lyrebirds are apparently in need of protection, which also encompasses the magpie larks, bell magpies and the butcherbirds, although the last two would be more correctly classed as carnivorous species.

In many areas where particularly choice species of insectivorous birds occur, there is a dearth of bird trappers who are prepared to handle the delicate species. Such an area is southeast Asia, particularly Malaysia, with the result that the insectivorous broadbills, e.g. the dusky and banded species, and many other birds are never available.

The Carnivorous Softbills

The Kingfishers

Kingfishers, particularly the carnivorous species, are usually avoided by aviculturists because of the supposed feeding problems which they present, which is a great pity as many are both colourful and easy to maintain. With one exception the carnivorous kingfishers are those which feed mainly upon fish, but also take other aquatic vertebrates and invertebrates. They are seldom exhibited, even in the larger zoological gardens. The exception is the kookaburra which feeds upon terrestrial vertebrates such as lizards, small snakes, birds and small mammals.

The fish-eating kingfishers are widespread and occur in both the New and Old Worlds. With the exception of the belted kingfisher, which is migratory and breeds in North America and winters in the West Indies and tropical America, the New World species are seldom seen in captivity. The belted kingfisher, like the larger ringed species, is a hovering bird; whilst on the continent of Africa the pied kingfisher similarly hovers above the water and plunges head first to capture fish. Other fishers, such as the giant, shining blue and malachite kingfishers scan the water from a suitable vantage point before diving, and when a fish is taken they immediately leave the water and return to the same perch.

The pied kingfisher also occurs in parts of southern Asia, from where the black-capped and the stork-billed kingfisher are occasionally available. The latter species is the largest of the colourful kingfishers and has the reputation of being an aggressive bird in the wild, attacking birds far larger than itself. However, a hand-reared specimen housed in a conservatory aviary with numerous smaller softbills never showed signs of such behaviour, but had the unusual habit when bathing of diving into the centre of a large pool, and then flapping clumsily to the side to clamber out. This was repeated several times, but surely cannot be characteristic of the wild bird or the species would not survive in areas where carnivorous fish, sharks, crocodiles and turtles abound.

Whereas the majority of insectivorous kingfishers nest in holes in trees, the carnivorous species are also hole-nesters but excavate tunnels, mainly in river banks. These tunnels often extend for several feet before they are enlarged to form the nest chamber. The giant kingfisher is said to have tunnels between 6 and 8 ft. long. None of the species use nesting material and lay their eggs upon the soil, which soon becomes littered with fish bones and scales.

The well known kookaburra or laughing jackass of the Australo-Papuan subregion is the only truly carnivorous terrestrial feeding kingfisher. It feeds upon whatever small vertebrates it is able to overpower, and venomous snakes are also included. As a destroyer of vermin and snakes the kookaburra is highly regarded in Australia, where it is a common bird due to the recent export ban. The other members of the small genus dacelo, to which the kookaburra belongs, are insectivorous.

The kookaburra and the giant kingfisher share the distinction of being the largest species of kingfishers, but neither species has the brilliant colouring normally associated with the kingfishers.

The Ground Hornbills

Although many of the larger arboreal hornbills include vertebrates—small mammals and reptiles, in their diet, the bulk of their food intake consists of fruit and insects. With the ground hornbills the reverse is the case, as they feed mainly upon frogs, small snakes and lizards, rats and mice and large insects. They are said to band together when tackling large snakes or monitor lizards. Like all hornbills they are hole nesters, but they do not seal up the nest entrance as do the other species. Their nesting sites are close to the ground in rotting trees or stumps, and sometimes even on the ground amongst boulders. The hen is said to leave the nest to feed, and the cock bird shares the incubating as well as feeding the young. The nestling period is reported to be at least 82 days, a surprisingly long time for helpless nestlings to be at the mercy of Africa's many predators.

The ground hornbills are restricted to Africa, where they occur south of the Sahara in the drier areas of sparsely wooded grassland and scrub. They are said to congregate at the edges of grass fires where they benefit from the myriad of small creatures endeavouring to escape from the heat and smoke. Due to the encroachment of civilisation they are decreasing in most parts of their range, and are sorely in need of protection.

They are frequently to be seen in the larger zoological gardens but cannot really be classed as a private aviculturist's bird. They should not be housed with any smaller species of bird, softbilled or otherwise, and are best kept on their own or in company with the bustards, cranes or large waterfowl.

The Roadrunners

The 2 species of roadrunner are aberrant members of the cuculidae family and are closely related to the ground cuckoos. They are restricted to the drier areas of the south-western United States of America and Mexico, hence their common American name of "chaparral cock"—the chaparral being the cacti and sage bush region of southern Arizona and New Mexico. They have very short wings and prefer to run when danger threatens or when they are pursuing their prey, and it has been estimated that they can attain a speed of 18 miles per hour.

They are handsome black and tan birds with a short crest and long tail, which they have the habit of cocking up in the manner of the toucans when roosting. They are well adapted for a terrestrial existence as their powerful legs and feet resemble those of the pheasants, and their wild diet consists of small lizards, snakes, mice and insects. Relatively large venomous snakes, including rattlesnakes, are occasionally tackled.

The roadrunners are not parasitic and for such a terrestrial species it is unusual that they should nest in bushes and trees, often as high as 16 ft. from the ground. Their young are helpless at birth, but are said to grow rapidly. An interesting feature of their nesting habits is that the eggs are laid at widely varying intervals, even though incubation commences after the first egg is laid. Consequently eggs are still being laid after the first egg has hatched, and the newly hatched chicks are then at the mercy of the more mature ones.

It is illegal to keep them in captivity in North America, and the few which find their way to the bird collections of the eastern hemisphere probably originate from Mexico.

The Shrikes
It seems reasonable to include the shrikes (which feed upon frogs, lizards, small birds and mice in addition to insects) with the carnivorous softbills, and of these they are the most readily available, although by no means plentiful. The Indian rufous-backed and grey shrikes are quite frequently offered by exporters but are normally of little interest to most aviculturists. The lesser grey shrike, fiscal shrike and grey-headed bush shrike are all African species which are said to include chameleons in their natural diet. The fiscal shrike is a most aggressive bird which boldly tackles any small vertebrates unable to defend themselves. They have been known to take nestlings of species as large as the bokmakierie shrike, and it is said that they startle caged birds into fluttering against the bars of their cages where they are seized and decapitated. The fiscal shrike is a common resident African species, and has become adapted to life around human habitation and plantations, whereas most species of carnivorous shrikes are denizens of the more open woods and grasslands of the Old World.

The shrikes are aggressive birds and their companions should be chosen from the medium sized softbills which themselves are hardly timid, for example the jay thrushes, mountain tanagers and the larger kingfishers. They should certainly not be housed with any birds, however large, if it is hoped to do any breeding.

Many species of shrike impale their prey upon thorns or any sharp projection, for later use; and as a result of this habit they are popularly known as butcher birds.

Appendix A

TABLE A1

The composition of some insects used for bird feeding

	Fat	Protein	Carbo-hydrate	Cal. per 100 gm.	Fibre	Mois-ture*	Calcium	Phos-phorus
Mealworms	12·0	20·8	1·86	204	2·0	61·9	0·03	0·27
Blowfly maggots	8·4	16·7	0·89	150	2·2	70·6	0·02	0·2
Blowflies	7·7	21·4	—	160	3·1	68·1	0·09†	0·72†
House Crickets	5·1	18·8	(not checked)			66·7	(not checked)	

Footnote to table:

* The moisture content is of freshly killed insects.

† The sample of blowflies analysed for calcium and phosphorus had dried out naturally and the moisture content was only 11·1% as opposed to 68·1% for freshly killed insects. As a higher moisture content would result in a lower calcium and phosphorus content, it can safely be assumed that the levels in freshly killed blowflies will be similar to that of the maggots and mealworms.

It will be seen that there are many times more phosphorus than calcium in these insects, even though both are present in minute quantities, whereas the reverse is the ratio required. Although the adult bird can probably mobilise approximately 25% of the calcium required for egg shell deposition from its body, the remainder would certainly not be supplied by these insects. Neither would sufficient phosphorus, as this would be present at the rate of only 0·23% of a diet comprising equal parts of maggots and mealworms. Nestlings would never be able to grow normally on such a low intake of calcium and phosphorus.

TABLE A2

The composition of some items used for bird feeding

	Fat %	Protein %	Carbo-hydrate %	Cal/ 100 g	Calcium mg	Phos-phorus mg	Vit A Iμ	Vit D Iμ	Vit B₁ mg	Vit B₂ mg	Nico-tinic acid mg	Vit C mg	Panto-thenic acid mg
Beef Dripping	99·0	tr	—	920·0	0·8	13·0	tr	tr	tr	tr	tr	tr	tr
Raw Beef	10·5	19·3	—	177·0	5·4	276·0	tr	tr	0·07	0·20	5·0	—	0·40
Raw Herring	15·1	16·7	1·5	273·0	101·0	272·0	150	900	0·03	0·30	3·5	tr	1·0
Cheese (Cheddar)	34·5	25·4	tr	425·0	810·0	545·0	1400	14	0·04	0·50	0·1	—	0·30
Shrimps	2·4	22·3	—	114·0	320·0	270·0	tr	tr	0·03	0·03	3·0	tr	0·30
Banana	tr*	1·1	19·2	77·0	6·8	28·1	0·20†	—	0·04	0·07	0·6	10·0	0·20
Apples (English)	tr	0·2	9·2	36·0	3·5	8·5	0·03†	—	0·04	0·02	0·1	5·0	0·07
Currants	tr	1·7	63·1	244·0	95·2	40·4	—	—	0·03	—	—	—	—
Dates	tr	2·0	63·9	248·0	67·9	63·8	0·05†	—	0·07	0·04	2·0	—	0·80
Grapes	tr	0·6	15·5	60·0	4·2	16·1	tr†	—	0·04	0·02	0·3	4·0	0·05
Melon	tr	1·0	5·3	24·0	19·1	30·4	2·00†	—	0·05	—	0·5	25·0	0·23
Orange	tr	0·8	8·5	35·0	41·3	23·7	0·05†	—	0·10	0·03	0·2	50·0	0·25
Pears	tr	0·2	10·4	40·0	6·9	9·5	0·01†	—	0·03	0·03	0·2	3·0	0·05
Sultanas	tr	1·7	64·7	249·0	52·2	94·6	tr†	—	0·10	—	—	—	—
Carrots (Boiled)	tr	0·9	4·5	21·0	28·8	29·5	9·00†	—	0·05	0·04	0·4	4·0	0·25
Tomatoes	tr	0·9	2·8	14·0	13·3	21·3	0·70†	—	0·06	0·04	0·6	20·0	0·05
Honey	tr	0·4	76·4	288·0	5·3	17·0	—	—	tr	0·05	0·2	tr	—

Footnote to table :

*Trace.

†Vitamin A is present in plant material in the form of carotene, which is converted into the vitamin in the wall of the gut, and is then stored in the liver. The figures given are mg per 100 g.

Vitamin K is adequately present in cereals.

Vitamin E is present in the oil of the germ of cereals, particularly wheat.

Appendix B

Proven Diets for Softbills

Hummingbirds

Most modern recipes for hummingbirds involve the use of a high protein food added to either a sugar or a honey solution. One such mixture which has had excellent results in maintaining these birds comprises Gevral Protein and white sugar in the ratio of 1 level teaspoon of the former to 4 level teaspoons of sugar. After the Gevral has been dissolved in warm water and the sugar in hot water, the mixture is made up to 5 fl. oz. In 1 oz. of Gevral there are 18 gm. of protein and 7 gm. of carbohydrate, and the calorie content is 105·3. In 1 oz. of white sugar there is only the merest trace of protein, no fat and 112 calories of carbohydrate. Therefore the calorific content of these food items is similar, the difference being that the calories in Gevral are mainly derived from protein, which will maintain the body; those derived from the sugar are of carbohydrate origin and will provide the required energy. It is important to remember that the latter calories will be present at the rate of almost 5 times the content of protein calories in the mixture described above. This intake has seemed satisfactory for individuals with relatively little space compared with their wild counterparts, and it has not produced an over-fat condition. In view of this it is likely that the hummingbird in the wild state has an even higher calorie intake to maintain its energy output.

In addition to the above diet insects should also be offered and the only species available in any quantity are of course drosophila. The Gevral Protein contains vitamins and mineral salts and it is therefore unnecessary to add these to the diet.

Other Nectivorous Birds

The sunbirds, flowerpeckers and the more exacting honey-creepers (the scarlet-thighed, yellow-bellied, blue, etc.) do not require the high carbohydrate content of hummingbird foods and such mixtures would be harmful to them in a very short time. Possibly a solution of 1 teaspoon of Gevral to 2 teaspoons of white sugar would be suitable as the carbohydrate content of this mixture would be just over half that of the humming-bird's diet. A food mixture which has produced excellent results is made up of 7 rounded teaspoons of both Complan and honey mixed with 20 oz. warm water. One oz. of Complan contains 8·8 gm. of protein, 4·6 gm. of fat and 12·5 gm. of carbohydrate, and the calorific value is 125 of which 36 are derived from the protein. One oz. of honey provides approximately 80 calories, all of which are from the carbohydrate content.

These birds should also receive fruit and insects as outlined in chapter 6. This also applies to the bananaquits, spider hunters and the less exacting honeycreepers (yellow-winged and black-headed honeycreepers,) except that a 1-part honey to 10 parts of water solution is sufficient for them. The protein, vitamin and mineral percentage of their food intake will be derived from the larger quantities of insects and insectile mixture that they should be allowed to consume.

The Frugivorous Softbills

Because of the similarity of requirements of all the frugivorous species there is little point in repeating the information concerning their nutrition which is contained in chapter 6. When they are housed in mixed collections however the availability of other foods, and the presence of their normal foods in larger quantity, will probably result in an individual variation of foods consumed. This of course is likely to happen with all birds in community aviaries, with the exception of the hummingbirds.

The Omnivorous Softbills

There is far greater variation of requirements among the omnivorous softbilled birds than in any other group, and the percentages of fruit, insects and insectile mixture outlined in chapter 6 should be closely followed. The diet suitable for birds at one extreme of this group (toucans, cocks of the rock etc.) would be unsuitable for those at the other end of the scale, i.e. the crows, red-billed hornbill etc. It is mainly a question of protein intake, as the toucans and their allies require little more than the truly frugivorous birds; whereas the meat, insects and insectile mixture required by the red-billed hornbill and crows, an insectivorous diet, is supplemented with fruit also.

The Insectivorous Softbills

For insectivorous birds that will accept inanimate foods an insectile mixture composed of the ingredients given in table B1. has been found suitable.

TABLE B1

Ingredients of a successful insectile mixture

16%	Plain biscuit meal
32%	Wholemeal flour
10%	Soya flour
10%	Coarse ground shrimp
12%	Fine ground shrimp
10%	Fish meal
10%	Meat and bone meal

To the mixture outlined in table B1 should be added a quantity of a good quality mineral salt and vitamin mixture.

The mixture is moistened with honey at the rate of 18 oz. per 50 oz. and is used in this state for the nectivorous birds, or is supplemented with raw minced beef at the rate of 1 part beef to 3 parts of the mixture (by volume) for the insectivorous and omnivorous species. For the more carnivorous birds (motmots, malcohas etc.), the percentage of meat is increased.

The composition of these mixtures before the addition of the mineral salt and vitamin supplement is given in table B2.

TABLE B2

Composition of insectile mixture outlined in table B1

	Basic mixture with honey (%)	Plus raw minced beef (%)
Oil	4·60	6·40
Crude protein	21·50	21·00
Calcium	1·07	0·71
Metabolisable energy	1258·00 cals/lb.	1082·00 cals/lb.
Crude Fibre	0·80	0·50
Phosphorus	1·00	0·76
Salt	0·76	0·55
Lysine	1·10	1·21
Methionine and cystine	0·65	0·74

In addition to the mixture given in table B1 the insectivorous species require ample live food daily, ranging from about 20% of the diet of the chats, niltavas, woodpeckers etc., to double that amount for the flycatchers, minivets, hoopoes, pittas etc.

The insectile mixture and added minced meat have been found unsuitable for the insectivorous kingfishers, and in addition to their live food requirements they should be given strips of meat and fish, and small whole fish (whitebait) and shrimps if possible.

Glossary

Arboreal. Relating to trees, i.e. birds which spend most of their time in trees, coming to the ground occasionally to feed or drink, but nesting and roosting above ground.

Aviculture. The practice of keeping wild birds in aviaries for the purpose of study and breeding.

Calories. Units of heat, used as a measure of energy turn-over in animals. If an individual requires 500 calories to maintain its daily energy output, it must be provided with food which would yield that amount of heat when burned. One gm. of protein provides 4·1 calories of heat, 1 gm. of carbohydrate yields 3·75 calories, and 1 gm. of fat 9·3 calories.

Canthaxanthin. A synthetic red pigment which has produced good results in maintaining the scarlet, red and pink feathering of aviary birds.

Carotene. The orange pigment which is synthesised by green plants and is present in parts where chlorophyll is absent, e.g. carrots and ripe tomatoes. It is converted into vitamin A in the liver.

Crepuscular. Relating to twilight. Birds which are most active at dusk and just before dawn.

Dimorphism, Sexual. Differences in appearance between a male and female of a species, age and season being equal.

Endemic. Birds restricted to a particular area, region etc.

Flight reflex. The force which is exerted to keep a bird at a "safe" distance from danger. The flight reflexes are reduced to a minimum, from the human aspect, when birds are hand-reared or tamed.

Gregarious. Relating to those species which live in flocks, both species specific and in company with other birds.

Indigenous. Referring to birds native or naturally occurring in a country, not introduced.

Invertebrates. Those species of animals which do not belong to the vertebrata. They therefore lack a vertebral column.

Invert sugar. A mixture of glucose and fructose which is present in honey and many sweet fruits. It is available commercially, and has been used in hummingbird mixtures instead of honey. It lacks the small amounts of ash and protein and the other sugars which are found in honey.

Metabolism. The chemical processes which occur within an organism, which involve the breaking down of organic material to release the energy necessary for activity.

Nidifugous. The term used to describe young birds which leave the nest immediately or soon after they hatch. They are therefore both precocial—capable of locomotion, and ptilo-paedic, i.e. covered with down. They are not softbilled birds.

Oxidation. The process whereby fats and oils in bird foods deteriorate when exposed to the air, resulting in vitamins A and E becoming slowly oxydised. ANTI-OXIDANTS such as Santoquin and B.T.H. can be used to reduce this oxydisation. Strangely, vitamin E is also an anti-oxidant if it is present in sufficient quantity before any oxydisation begins.

Pathogenic organism. Parasites having the power to cause disease.

Polymorphism. A term used to denote the existence of several plumage phases within one interbreeding population independent of age, sex, season or race.

Symbiotic bacteria. Bacteria which are in association with a dissimilar organism, i.e. the bird, to their mutual advantage.

Synthesise. To put together a material in the body synthetically. It need therefore not be present in the diet. For example, the scarlet cock of the rock cannot synthesise the scarlet colouring unaided, and colour holding or producing agents must be present in the diet.

Terrestrial. Referring to those birds which spend most of the daylight hours upon the ground, even to the extent of nesting either at ground level or very low in bushes or undergrowth.

Several terrestrial species roost in trees or bushes, as a safety measure, e.g. pittas.

Torpidity. The term used to describe the time of inactivity and lowered body temperature, which enables such species as the hummingbirds to conserve energy and survive during periods of fasting, i.e. whilst roosting. A period of hibernation for longer periods is said to occur in the nightjars.

Vertebrates. All animals, i.e. birds, reptiles, mammals etc. which have a vertebral column.

Zoogeographical zones. The 6 major and 1 minor zones which completely divide the earth into separate animal areas determined mainly by climate, and the effect this has upon the particular conditions to which birds are adapted. For example the Ethiopian region, which is Africa south of the Sahara, and which is separated from the palaearctic region by the desert and from the neotropical and Australasian regions by the Atlantic and Indian Oceans.

Bibliography

BANNERMAN, D. A. *The Birds of West and Equatorial Africa.* Vol. 2; Oliver and Boyd. Edinburgh 1952.

BOND, J. *Birds of the West Indies*, Collins. London 1960.

GLENISTER, A. G. *Birds of the Malay Peninsula, Singapore and Penang.* Oxford Univ. Press. London 1951.

McCANCE, R. A., and WIDDOWSON, E. M. *The Composition of Foods*, H.M.S.O. London 1960.

MEYER DE SCHAUENSEE, R. *The Birds of Colombia.* Livingstone Pub. Co. Narberth, Penn. 1964.

RAND, A. L., and GILLIARD, E. T. *Handbook of New Guinea Birds.* Weidenfeld and Nicholson. London 1967.

RATCLIFFE, H. L. "The Use of Whalemeat at the Philadelphia Zoo." Personal communication, 1965.

ROBERTS, A. *Birds of South Africa.* "Cape Times." Cape Town 1961.

ROOTS, C. G. *Maggots and Mealworms.* Avic. Mag., Vol. 74, No. 5, 1968.

SKUTCH, A. F. *The Life History of the Prong-billed Barbet.* Auk 61, 1944.

SMYTHIES, B. E. *The Birds of Borneo.* Oliver and Boyd. London 1964.

THOMSON, A. LANDSBOROUGH. (ed.). *A New Dictionary of Birds.* Nelson. London/McGraw-Hill. New York 1964.

General Index

DESCRIPTIONS OF SPECIES ILLUSTRATED

Silver-throated Tanager
A hardy species which can be housed out of doors throughout the year once acclimatised, provided it has access to a draught-proof shelter. It is one of the most common species, in the wild and in captivity, but is always popular due to its attractive colour scheme.

Toucan Barbet
Like many of the larger barbets this bird cannot be trusted where smaller species or breeding birds are concerned. It is only occasionally received in importations from South America, but is always eagerly sought by aviculturists.

Pied Hornbill
A regularly imported Indian species the Pied Hornbill is one of the medium sized members of the family, and its companions must be chosen with care. Under normal garden conditions it should be given an aviary to itself, but in very large quarters its companions should be selected from the pheasants, toucans, imperial fruit pigeons etc.

Fairy Bluebird
The Fairy Bluebird is undoubtedly the most attractive of the readily available, low priced softbills. It is easy to maintain, is not aggressive towards smaller birds, and has bred on numerous occasions in captivity.

Lesser Green Broadbill

The only broadbill available to aviculturists, it can be treated as a standard omnivorous softbill. A good insectile mixture, soft fruits and a few mealworms occasionally will maintain it in good condition. The other species are highly insectivorous, some even being insect hawkers.

Red-headed Manakin

Few of these gems from the humid forests of Amazonia reach Europe alive, due to the difficulty most trappers appear to have in establishing them. Manakins are always scarce in collections but actually thrive when provided with a correct diet, which must include animal protein.

Blue-winged Siva

An insectivorous species from South East Asia the Blue-winged Siva is frequently imported and is usually relatively low in price. It is inoffensive and can safely be housed with other small softbills such as tanagers and honeycreepers.

Black-fronted Bush Shrike

There are several colour phases of this attractive bird and it is therefore said to show poymorphism. It is related to the shrikes and is of course highly insectivorous, and will not thrive in captivity unless provided with a high protein replacement mixture and ample live food.

Yellow-winged Honeycreeper

This is the most attractive species of honeycreeper and fortunately is readily available on the bird market, usually at a reasonable price. Nectar and soft fruit form the basis of their diet, but a good quality insectile mixture and a little live food should also be provided.

Scarlet Cock of the Rock
The bird most likely to attract attention wherever it is housed and however colourful its companions. Generally aggressive to smaller birds, it has proved possible to include it in a mixed collection provided ample space and cover are available. They are usually quite tame when first imported as the majority are taken from the nest for hand-rearing.

Sulphur-breasted Toucan
This species is the most frequently available large toucan, although the smaller aracaris and toucanets are often as plentiful. They should only be housed with large softbills such as jays, jay thrushes, fruit pigeons and similar birds which are able to defend themselves if necessary. A diet of fruit alone is insufficient and they must be treated as om-nivorous birds with a definite need for animal protein.

Spotted-Morning Warbler
A relative of the thrushes not the warblers, this species has been imported on several occasions in recent years from East Africa. They are insectivorous and inoffensive and have nested in captivity, small cup-shaped structures of mud and fibres being built on top of broken boughs. Their eggs are pale blue.

White-headed Touraco
This attractive species has proved to be harmless in tropically planted aviaries, whereas the common green species such as Schalows and Knysna Touracos are often destructive to the foliage. Although basically a frugivorous bird in the wild state, it should not be confined to a diet of cultivated fruit alone in captivity, as most of these provide little more than expensive water.

Van Den Bock's Pitta
A rare species from south east Asia this beautiful bird has appeared on importers' lists with increasing frequency in the last two years, and can now be seen in most bird collections worth the name, and in many private collectons too. Its superb colouring and bearing thoroughly justify its popularity.

Red-fronted Barbet

An East African barbet, this species is easy to maintain and should be given thick, rotten branches to drill into. Several holes are usually made and will almost certainly be used for roosting. It is an inoffensive species, unlike many of its relatives, and can be kept with a mixed collection of small softbills with impunity.

Spreo Starling

The most colourful of the regularly imported African glossy starlings this species has bred in captivity on a number of occasions. It is a hardy bird which thrives on the standard omnivorous softbill fare, and can safely be wintered out if the necessary precautions are taken.

Scaly-crowned Malcoha

An unusual ground cuckoo from the Philippines, it is non-parasitic and rears its own young. It roosts in trees but spends most of the daylight hours searching for food on the forest floor. All the Malcohas are highly carnivorous and need regular supplies of mice and other forms of fur and feather, but it must be remembered that they are not equipped to tear their prey, and food must be given in pieces which they can swallow whole.

Blue-winged Pitta

Pittas must always be provided with an earth floor and logs to perch on. Although they roost in trees they are otherwise terrestrial in their habits, and if kept on a hard and abrasive surface, such as concrete, they will certainly suffer from foot troubles.

Pileated Jay

A common South American species which should be housed with birds at least of equal size. They must have plenty of roughage, in the form of young mice and day old chicks, which they are quite capable of tearing apart themselves. A coarse insectile mixture should also be given, plus a little fruit.

Yellow-throated Longclaw
This attractive East African pipit has been imported into the British Isles several times in recent years. It has a rather nervous disposition and takes longer than most birds to accept captivity. Mainly terrestrial in habits, and of course highly insectivorous, it should be provided with an earth floor. Small seeds are also eaten.

Magpie Jay
A distinctive resident of the arid regions of Central America, Magpie Jays show the aggressive tendancies typical of members of the crow family and should not be kept with smaller birds. Toucans, small hornbills, jay thrushes and similar sized species will be safe in their company.

Greater Rufous Motmot
The most impressive of the motmots, and like all of them relatively easy to maintain once established. They are hardy birds which can be safely wintered out, provided they have access to a dry, draught free shelter. If their aviary has an earth floor they will almost certainly burrow, and will no doubt roost in one of their tunnels.

Black-headed Honeycreeper
The most aggressive honeycreeper, particularly against individuals of the same species, and it is seldom possible to keep more than one pair per aviary however sizeable this may be. Their short beaks signify a more insectivorous diet than the Yellow-winged species, and they have been maintained on fruit, insectile mixture and live food without receiving nectar.

White-collared Kingfisher
A widespread species from the Old World tropics, this kingfisher is the commonest of the family in captivity, where it has bred several times. Contrary to popular belief they, and many other species of kingfishers, are easy to maintain, and are seldom aggressive to other birds.

Woodland Kingfisher
Like the White-collared Kingfisher this is a 'forest' kingfisher,
a name used to indicate that it is not a fishing species. Insects,
lizards and amphibians form the bulk of its diet and it is
therefore easy to provide for in captivity. Although it often
occurs in the vicinity of water it nests in trees in natural holes
and the abandoned holes of barbets and woodpeckers.

Princess Wood Nymph Hummingbird
An attractive species from Ecuador, this is only one of many
hummingbirds imported annually into the British Isles. In a
few importers' establishments it is possible to make your
choice from perhaps twenty species. Their nutritional requirements have been the subject of research and controversy in
recent years, and suitable foods can be purchased commercially.

Brown-hooded Kingfisher
This easily kept, inoffensive kingfisher thrives on live food,
strips of raw meat and fish and small mice, and is ideal for a
community aviary. Like many birds from East Africa it is
never plentiful in aviculture.

D'Arnauds Barbet
An attractive and inexpensive species, D'Arnauds Barbet has
often been housed with tanagers, honeycreepers and other
small softbills without causing trouble. They tunnel, like all
barbets, but should be kept in an aviary with a natural floor
as they dig vertically into the soil.

Dollarbird
A typical aerial species, showing the broad bill of the insect
hawker, the long powerful wings for graceful flight and the
small feet which characterise the rollers. This bird has been
imported from tropical Asia in recent years and obviously
requires a great deal of space in captivity.

Violet Euphonia
A commonly available small tanager from northern South America. It will thrive on the standard omnivorous softbill diet of finely diced mixed fruit, a good quality insectile mixture and a little live food.

Necklaced Laughing Thrush
A large, attractively marked thrush from India, it is frequently imported and is usually inexpensive. Like all the members of its group however it has aggressive tendencies, and is a menace to nesting birds, small inoffensive species and injured specimens.

Orange Ground Thrush
Terrestrial in habits, this species will make full use of the aviary floor, so often wasted in a collection of softbilled birds. It is inclined to be aggressive to smaller ground-dwellers—Chats for instance—as it is highly territorial.

Scaly-Feathered Malkoha
Hailing from the Phillipine Islands this species is one of the most attractive of the Ground Cuckoos, none of which are available with the frequency that their colour and activity warrants. It is not parasitic, nor aggressive towards birds half its size, and its captive diet should include ample roughage in the form of chicks and mice. It is not equipped to deal with these whole however.

Abyssinian Ground Thrush
A rare species from East Africa which is far less terrestrial than the Asiatic Ground Thrushes, and spends a lot of time perching amongst the foliage. It is a non-aggressive species and is easily maintained on the standard Softbill diet.

Greater Rufous Motmot
One of the many species belonging to the order Coraciiformes which nest in holes in the ground, normally in river banks or mounds of earth. In captivity, when kept over soil, they will excavate several tunnels which are used for roosting. Leaves,

grass and feathers are taken down to line the enlarged chamber
at the end of the tunnel. They are easy to maintain in captivity,
but they are seldom good travellers when first imported.

Stork Billed Kingfisher

The most colourful of the larger species of Kingfishers the
Stork-billed species has a reputation of being a very aggressive
bird in the wild. It is a truly carnivorous Softbill, and aquatic
vertebrates form the bulk of its diet. The specimen in this
photograph has never lived up to its reputation and has lived
peacefully with many smaller Softbills. The eggs of Sunbitterns and Roulrouls lying in open view were not harmed by
this bird. Its liking for small mice no doubt indicates that
small water-frequenting mammals are included in the diet of
the wild bird.

White-Browed Blue Flycatcher

An attractive Asiatic species which occasionally arrives in
shipments of insectivorous species. It is rather more delicate
than the more commonly available Verditer and Tickell's
Flycatchers, and requires a higher temperature and more
live food.

Black-Fronted Bush Shrike

An extremely insectivorous species which can be meated off
but will not thrive on the standard Softbill diet. Unless large
coarse bodied insects such as locusts and crickets are regularly
supplied it is unlikely that this species will thrive.

Four Kingfishers which are occasionally imported and are
quite easy to maintain. From the dietary point of view the
Pygmy Kingfisher is the most exacting, as it usually will not
accept inanimate foods. The Brown-hooded Kingfisher, the
White-collared Kingfisher and the Angola Kingfisher readily
accept strips of meat and small fish in addition to live food.
None of these birds are aggressive towards Softbills of equal
size.